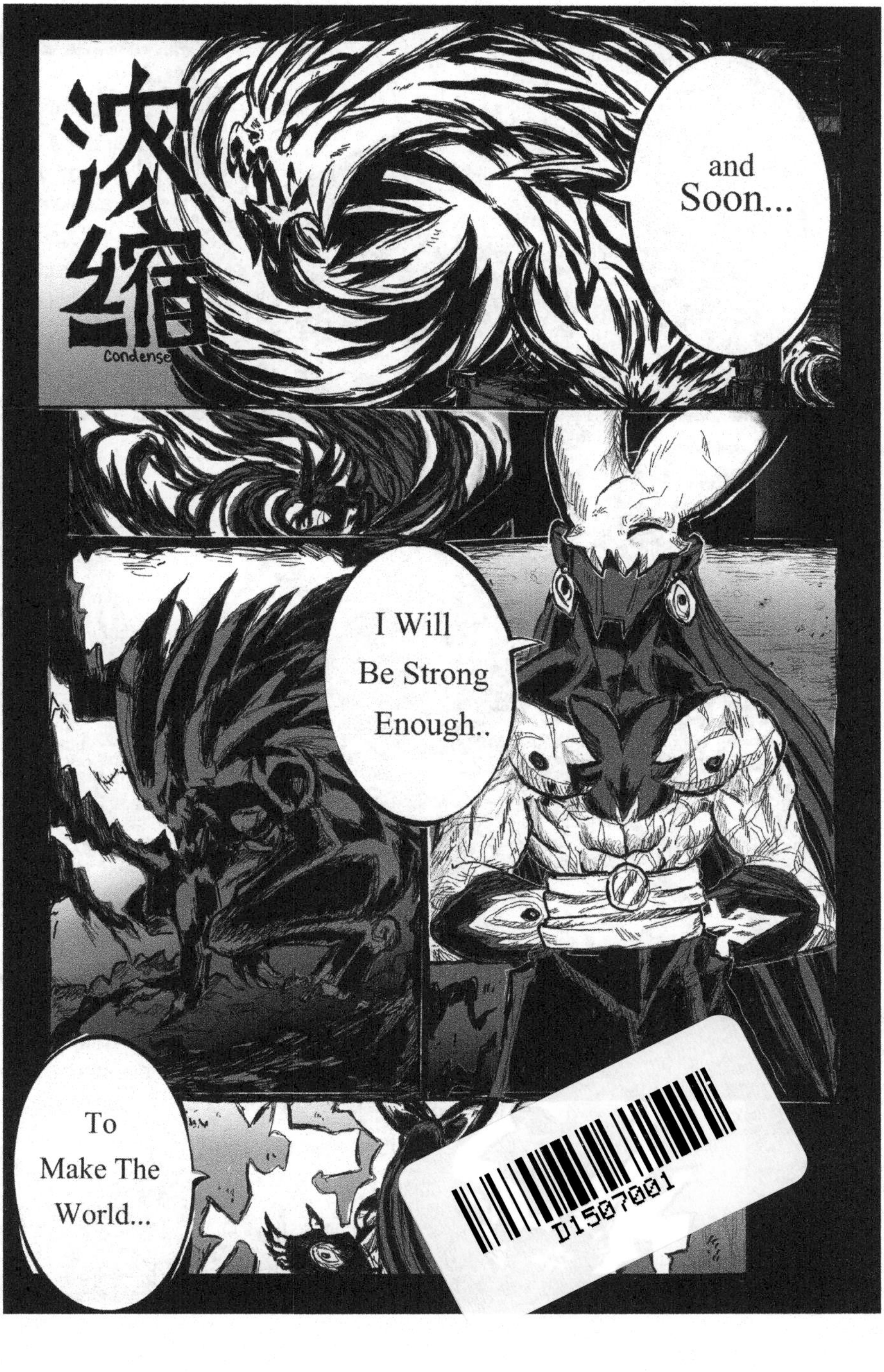

浓缩
condense
and Soon...
I Will Be Strong Enough..
To Make The World...

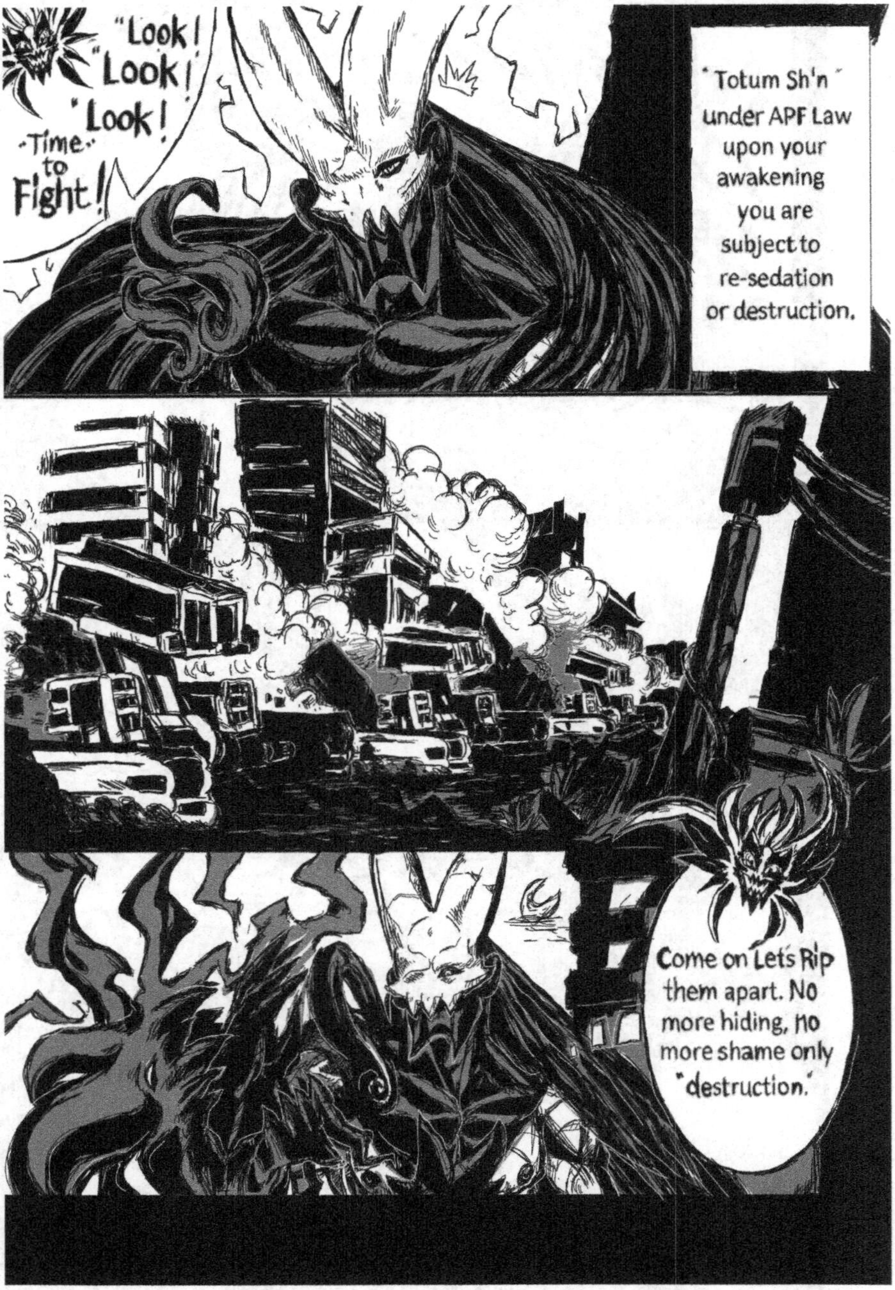
"Look!
"Look!
"Look!
-Time- to Fight!
"Totum Sh'n" under APF Law upon your awakening you are subject to re-sedation or destruction.
Come on Let's Rip them apart. No more hiding, no more shame only "destruction."

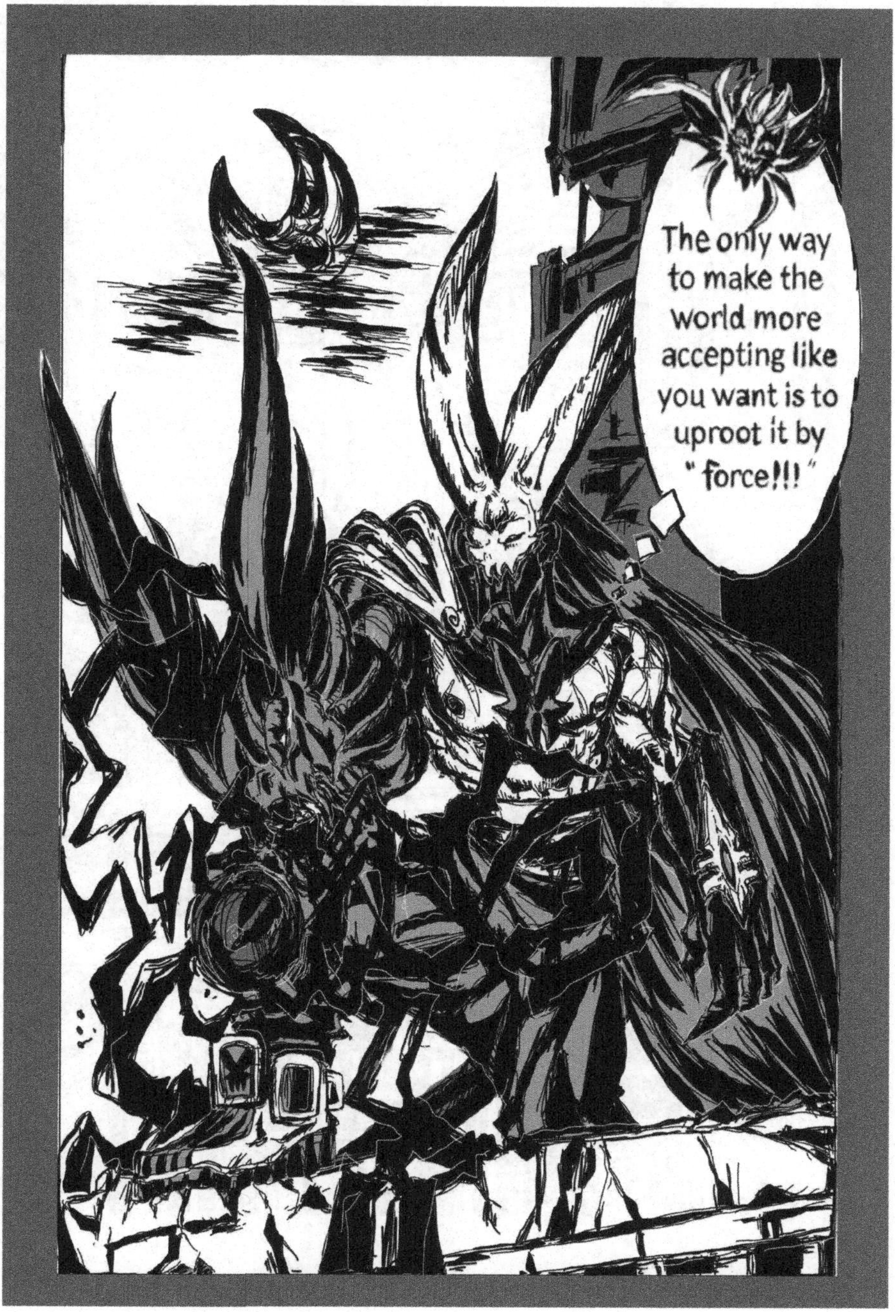
The only way to make the world more accepting like you want is to uproot it by " force!!! "

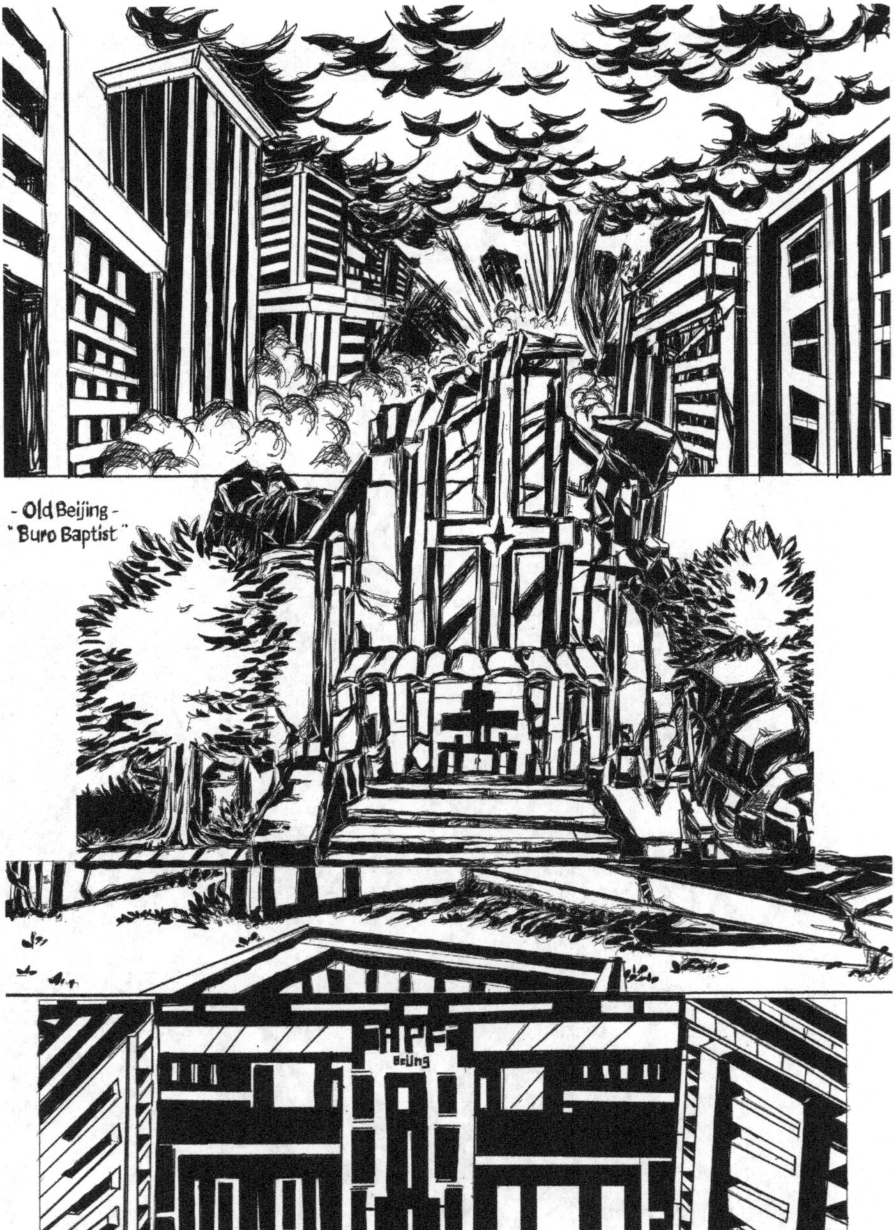
- Old Beijing -
"Buro Baptist"
APF
Beijing

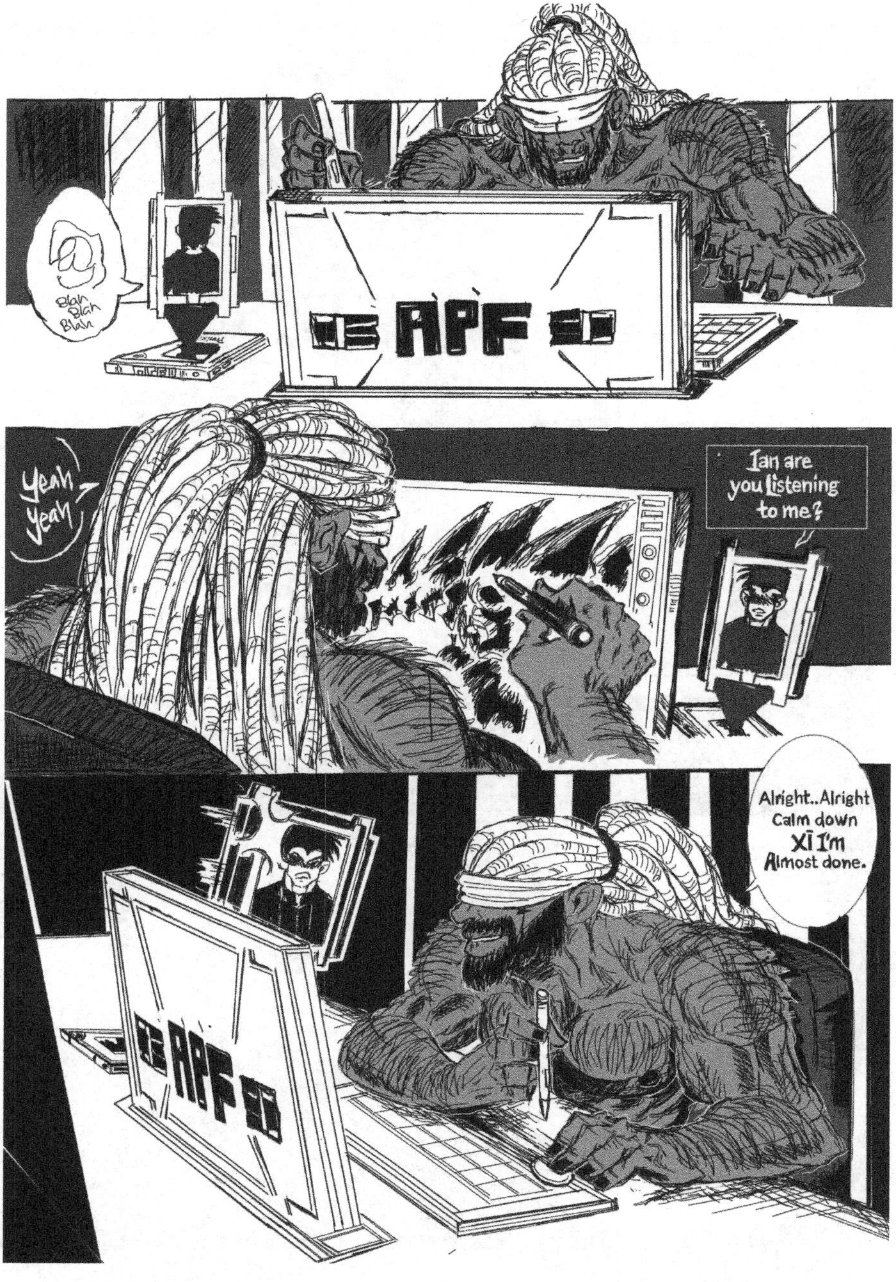
Blah Blah Blah
APF
Yeah yeah
Ian are you Listening to me?
Alright..Alright Calm down XI I'm Almost done.
APF

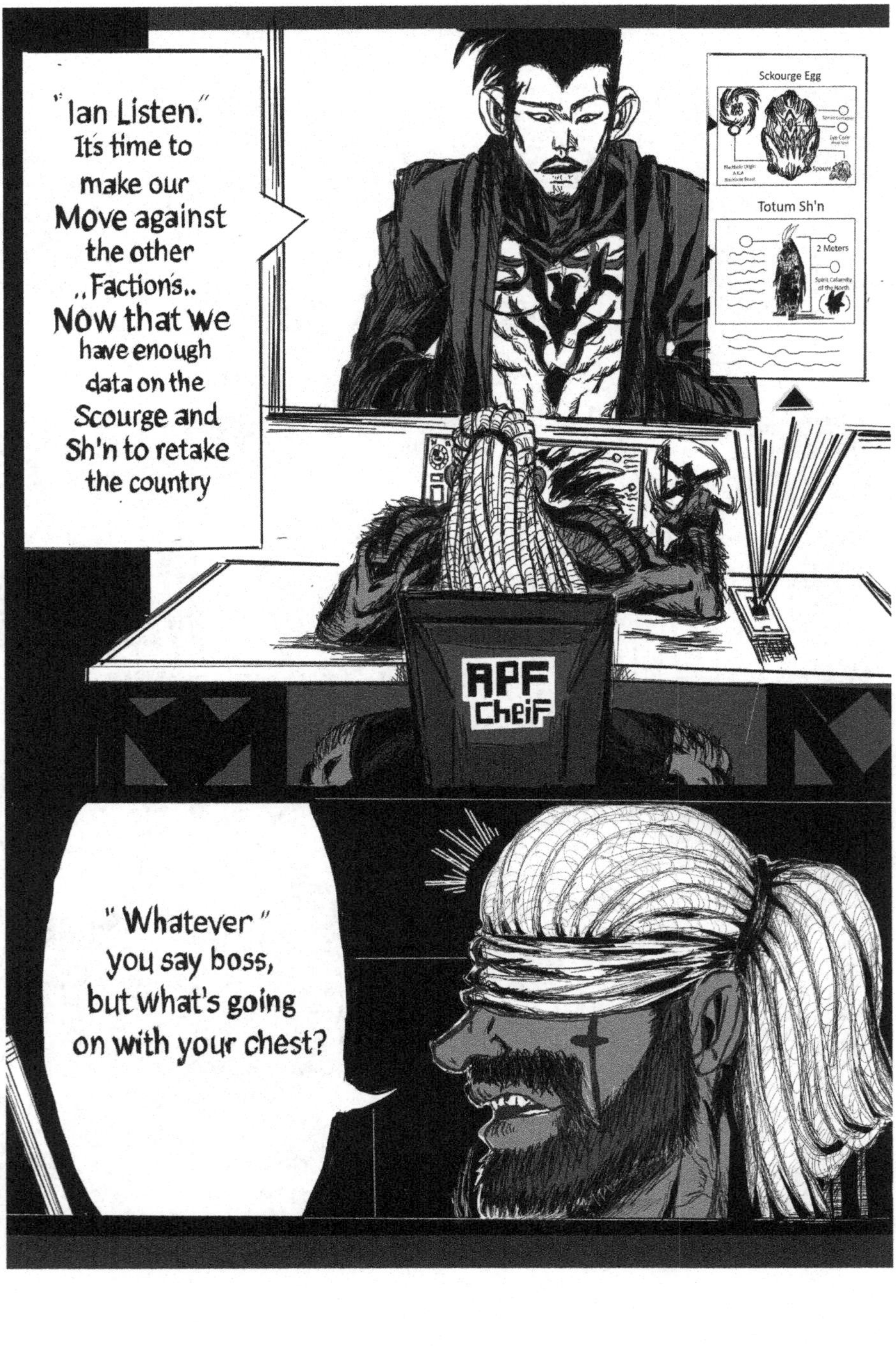
"Ian Listen." It's time to make our Move against the other ..Faction's.. Now that we have enough data on the Scourge and Sh'n to retake the country
Sckourge Egg
Eye Core
Spoure
Totum Sh'n
2 Meters
APF Cheif
"Whatever" you say boss, but what's going on with your chest?

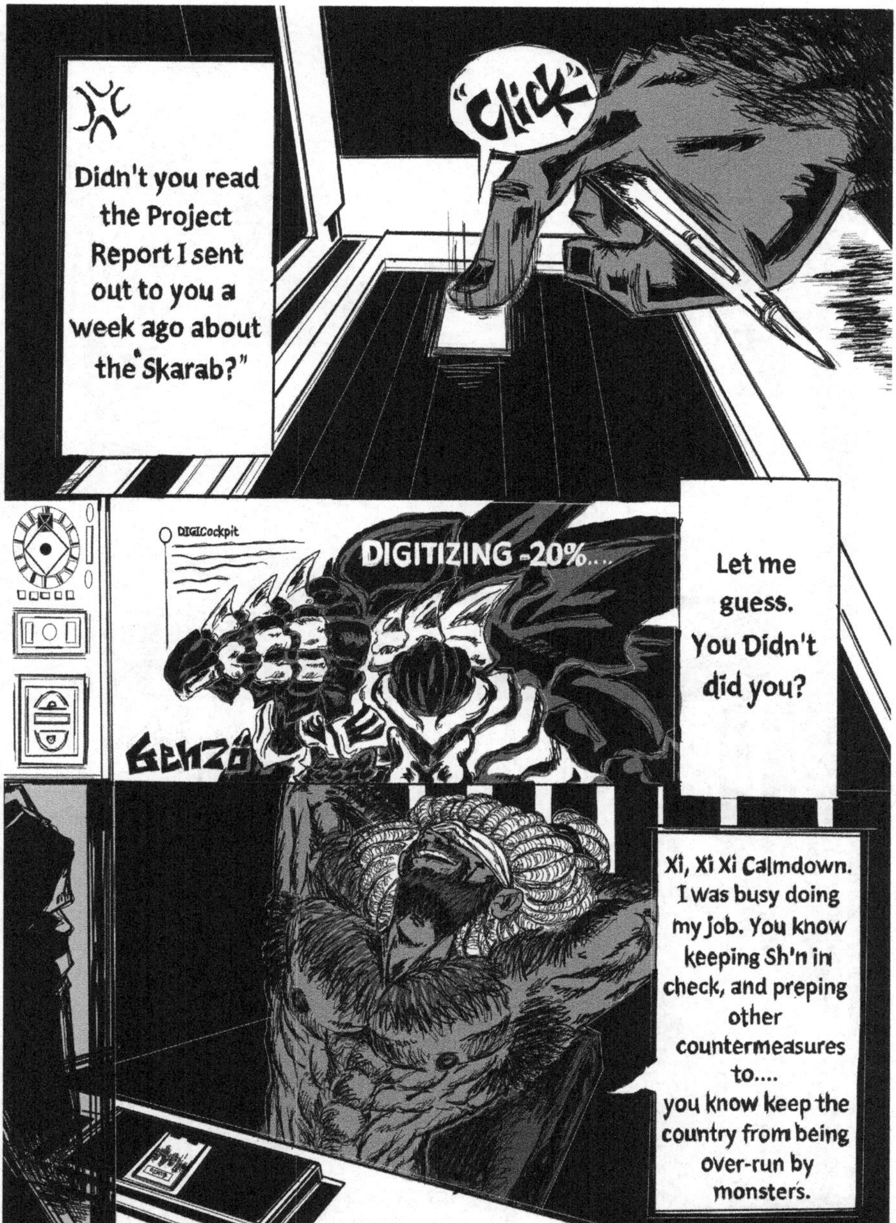
Didn't you read the Project Report I sent out to you a week ago about the "Skarab?"
"Click"
DIGICockpit
DIGITIZING -20%...
Genzo
Let me guess. You Didn't did you?
Xi, Xi Xi Calmdown. I was busy doing my job. You know keeping Sh'n in check, and preping other countermeasures to.... you know keep the country from being over-run by monsters.

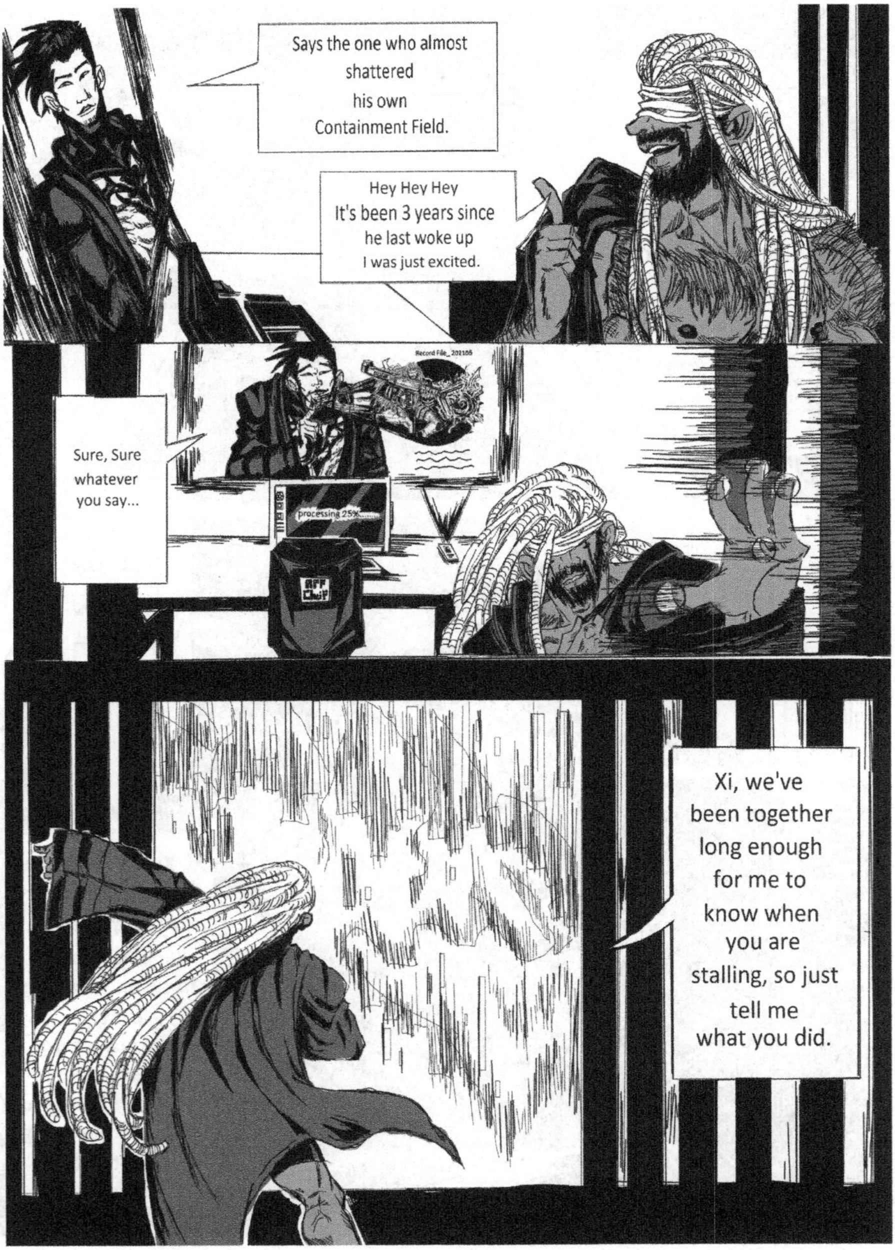
Says the one who almost shattered his own Containment Field.
Hey Hey Hey It's been 3 years since he last woke up I was just excited.
Record File_ 202105
Sure, Sure whatever you say...
processing 25%........
RFF Chip
Xi, we've been together long enough for me to know when you are stalling, so just tell me what you did.

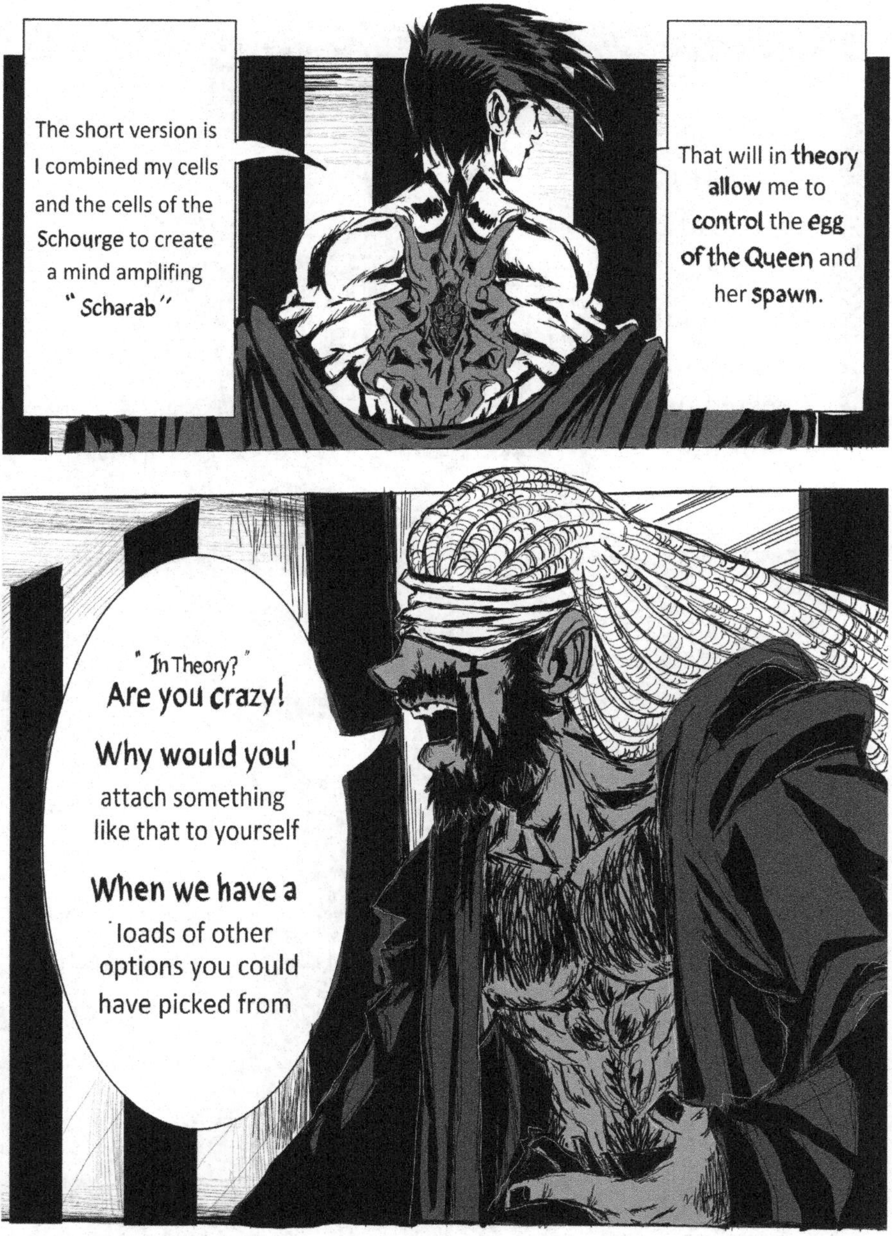

The short version is I combined my cells and the cells of the Schourge to create a mind amplifing " Scharab "
That will in theory allow me to control the egg of the Queen and her spawn.
" In Theory? " Are you crazy! Why would you' attach something like that to yourself When we have a loads of other options you could have picked from

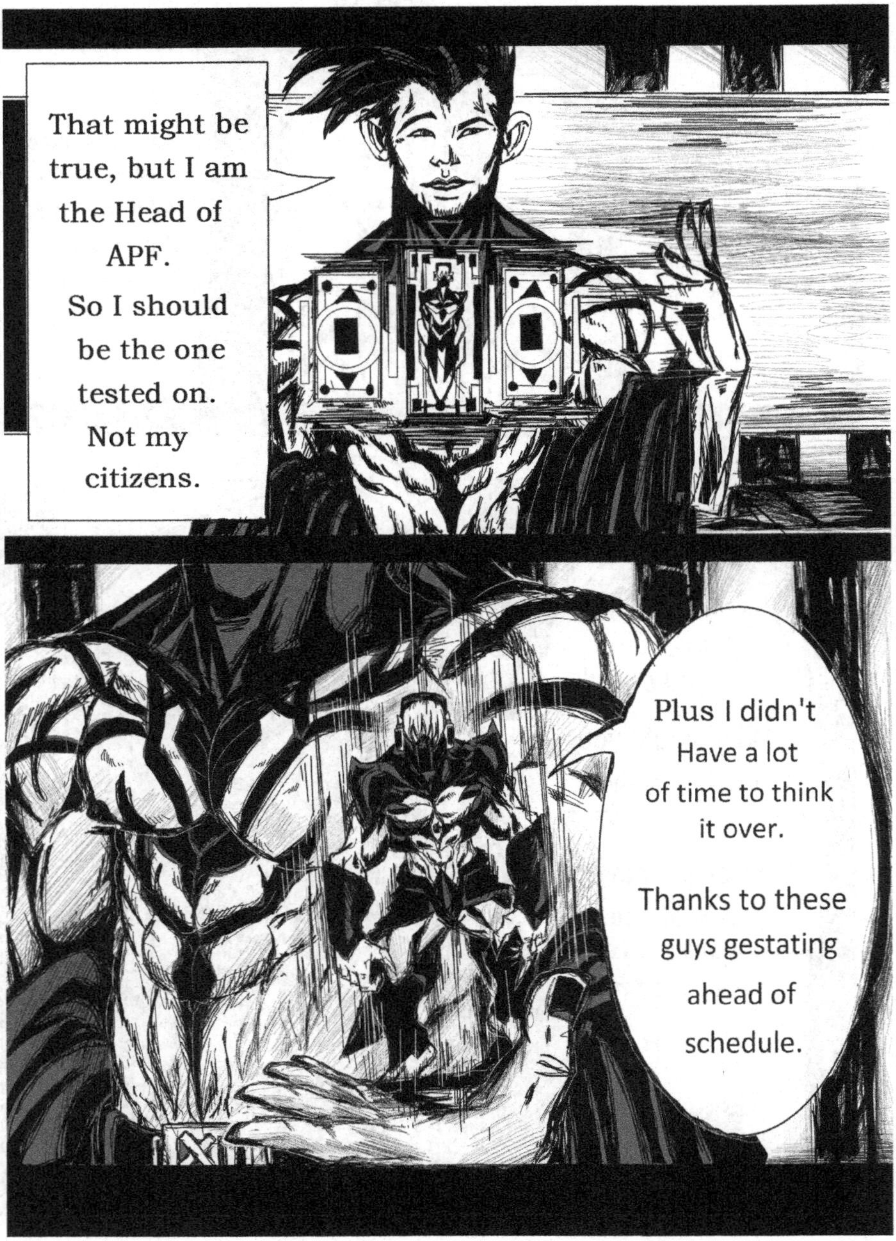
That might be true, but I am the Head of APF.
So I should be the one tested on.
Not my citizens.
Plus I didn't Have a lot of time to think it over.
Thanks to these guys gestating ahead of schedule.

APF Exterior Facility

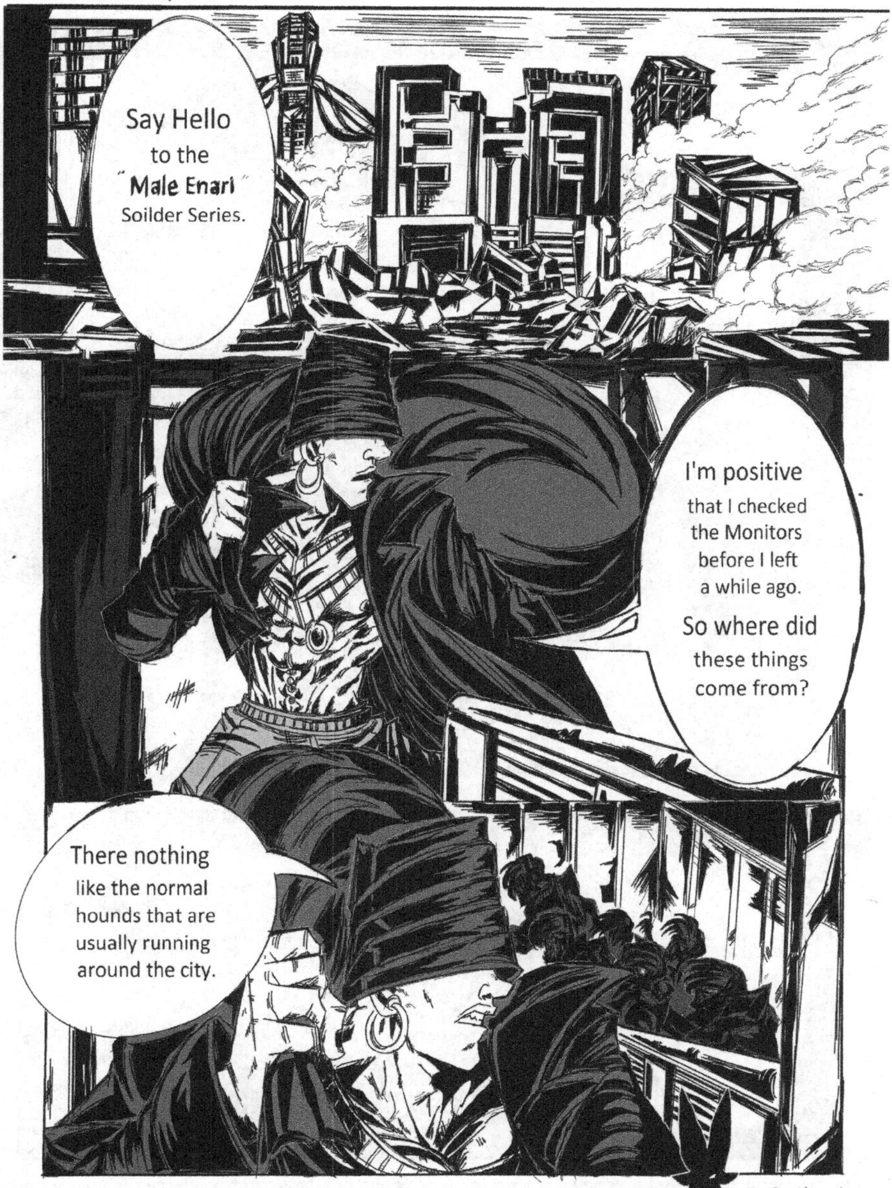
Say Hello to the "Male Enari" Soilder Series.
I'm positive that I checked the Monitors before I left a while ago. So where did these things come from?
There nothing like the normal hounds that are usually running around the city.

To Be Continued

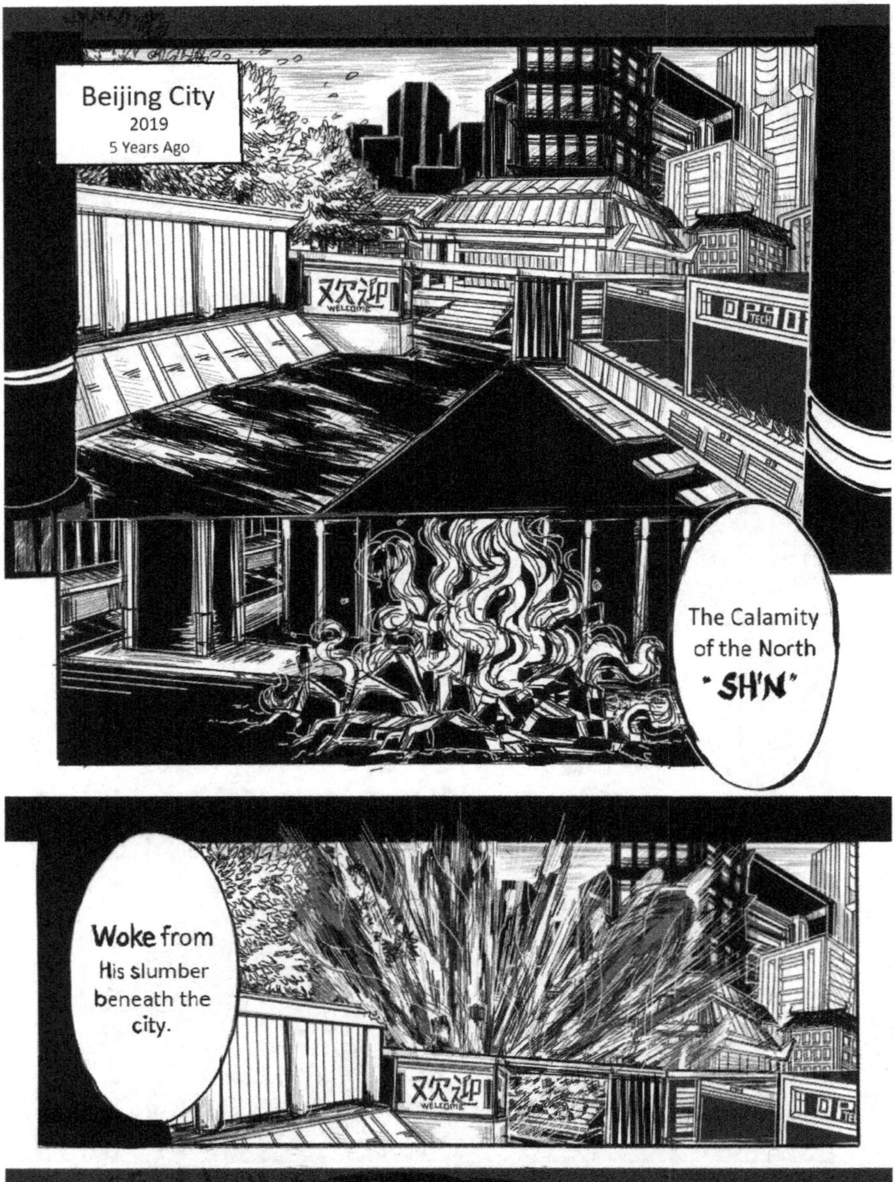
Beijing City
2019
5 Years Ago
欢迎
WELCOME
The Calamity of the North "SH'N"
Woke from His slumber beneath the city.

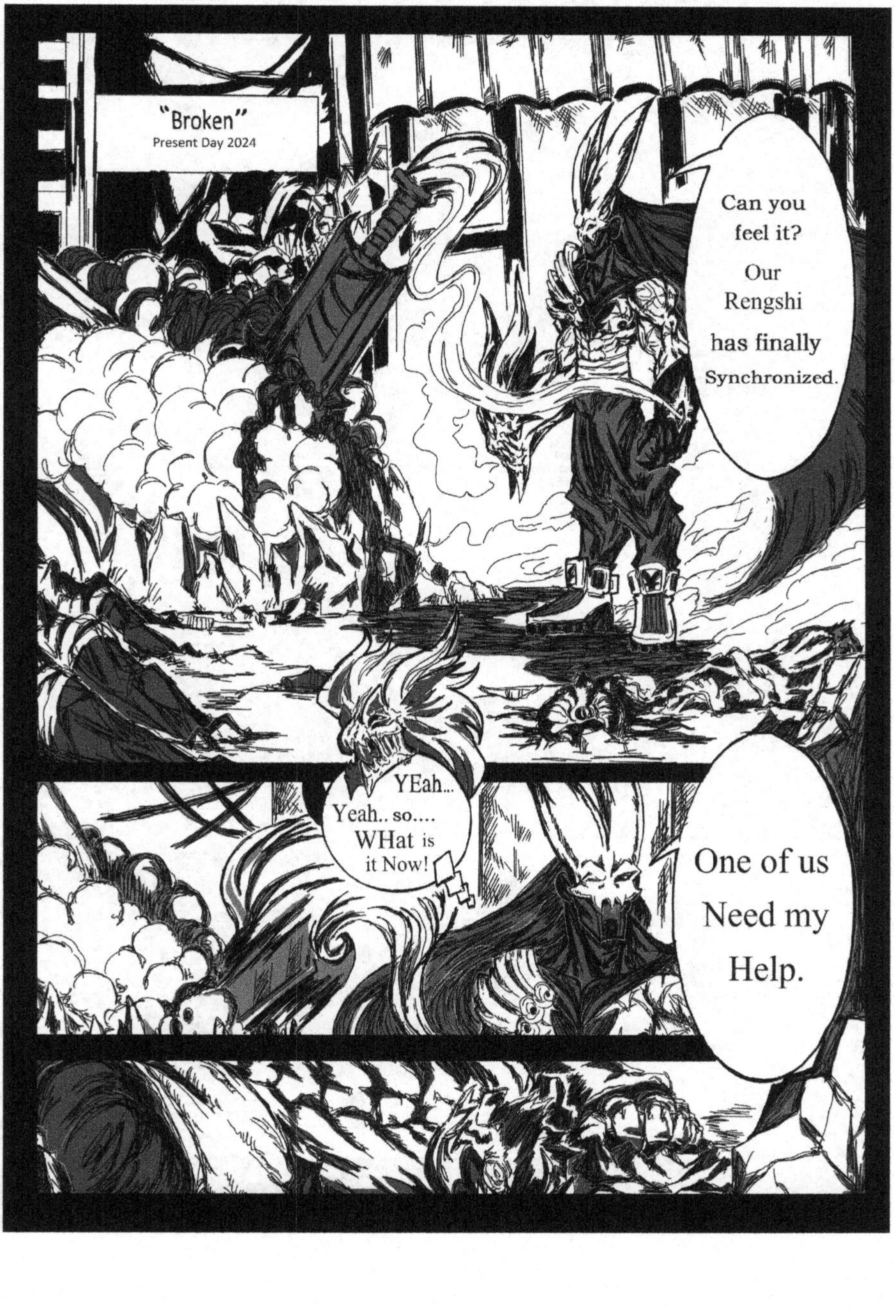
"Broken"
Present Day 2024
Can you feel it? Our Rengshi has finally Synchronized.
YEah...
Yeah.. so.... WHat is it Now!
One of us Need my Help.

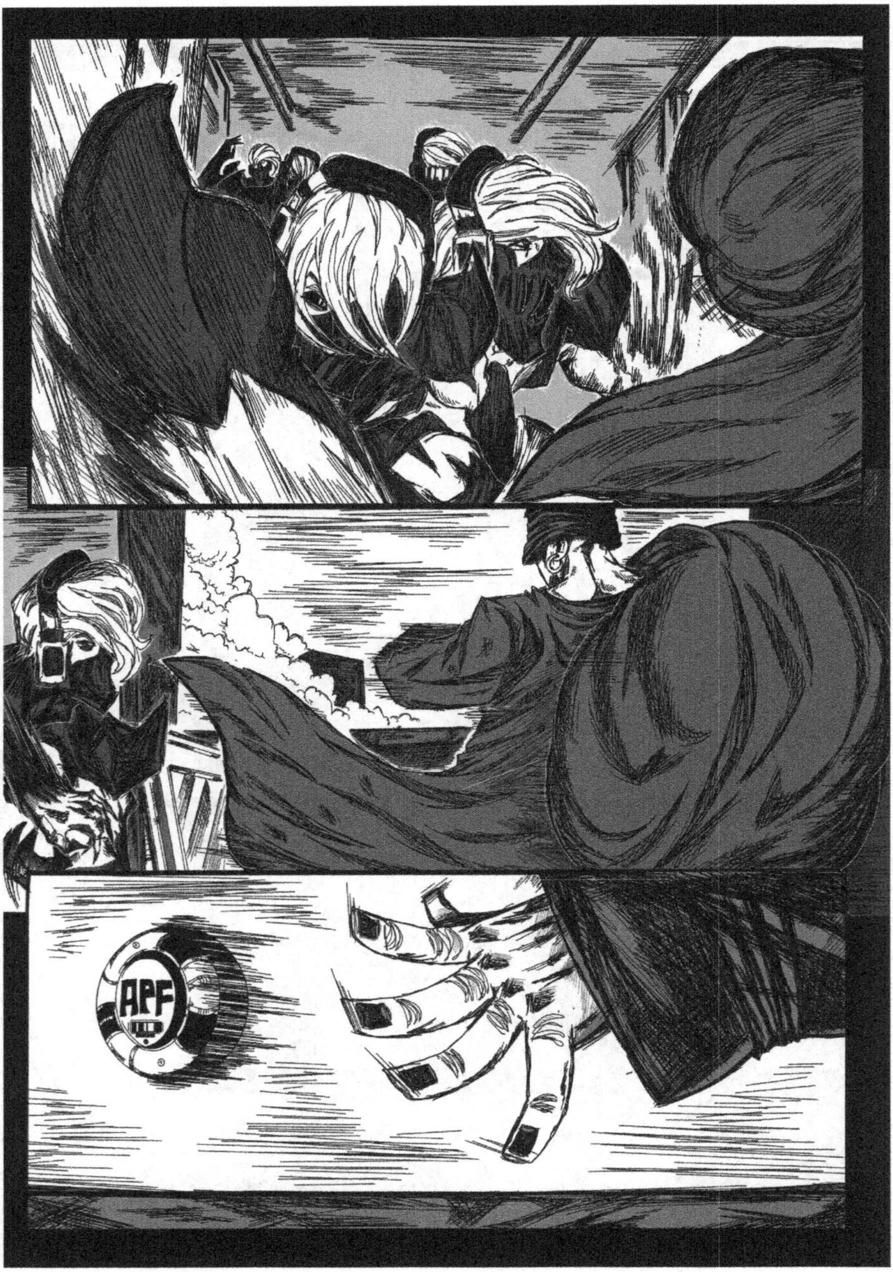
APF

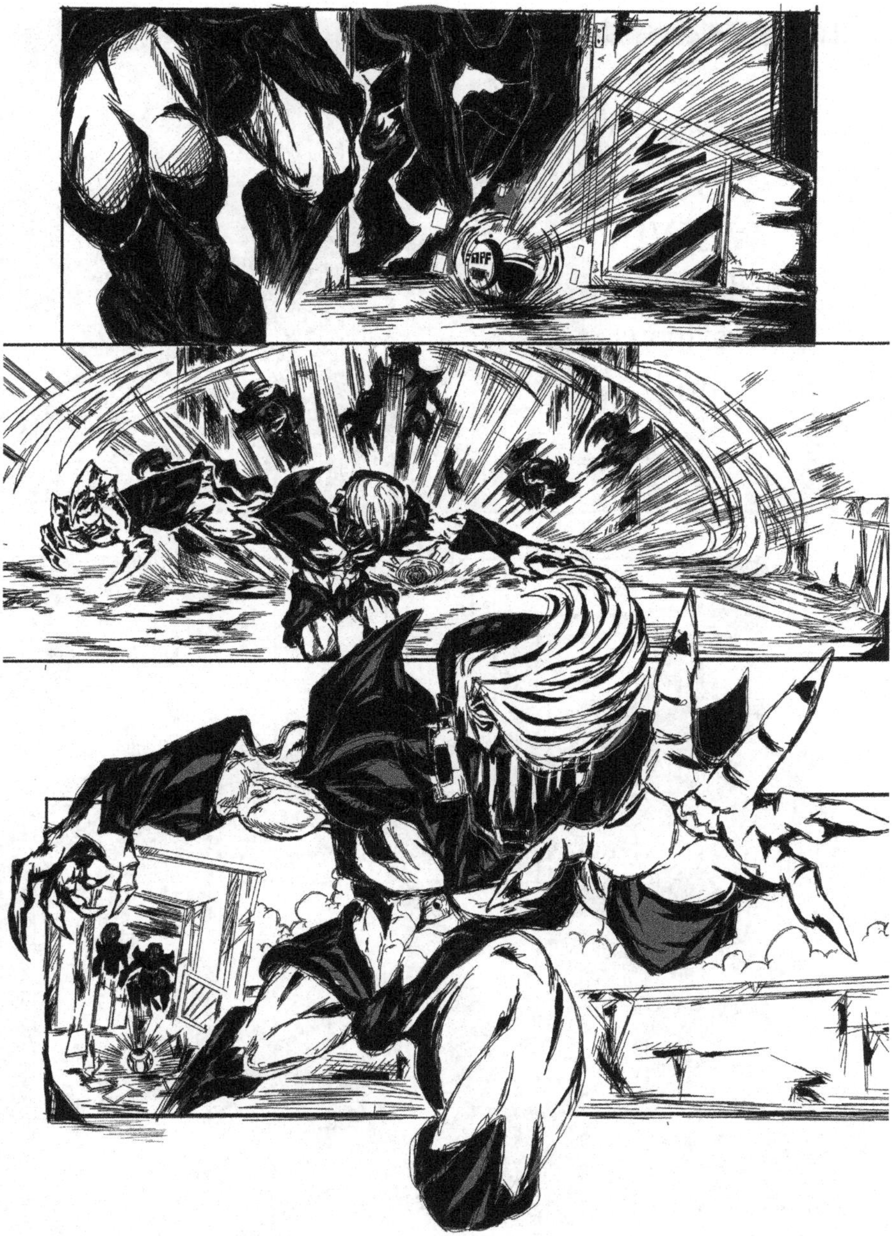

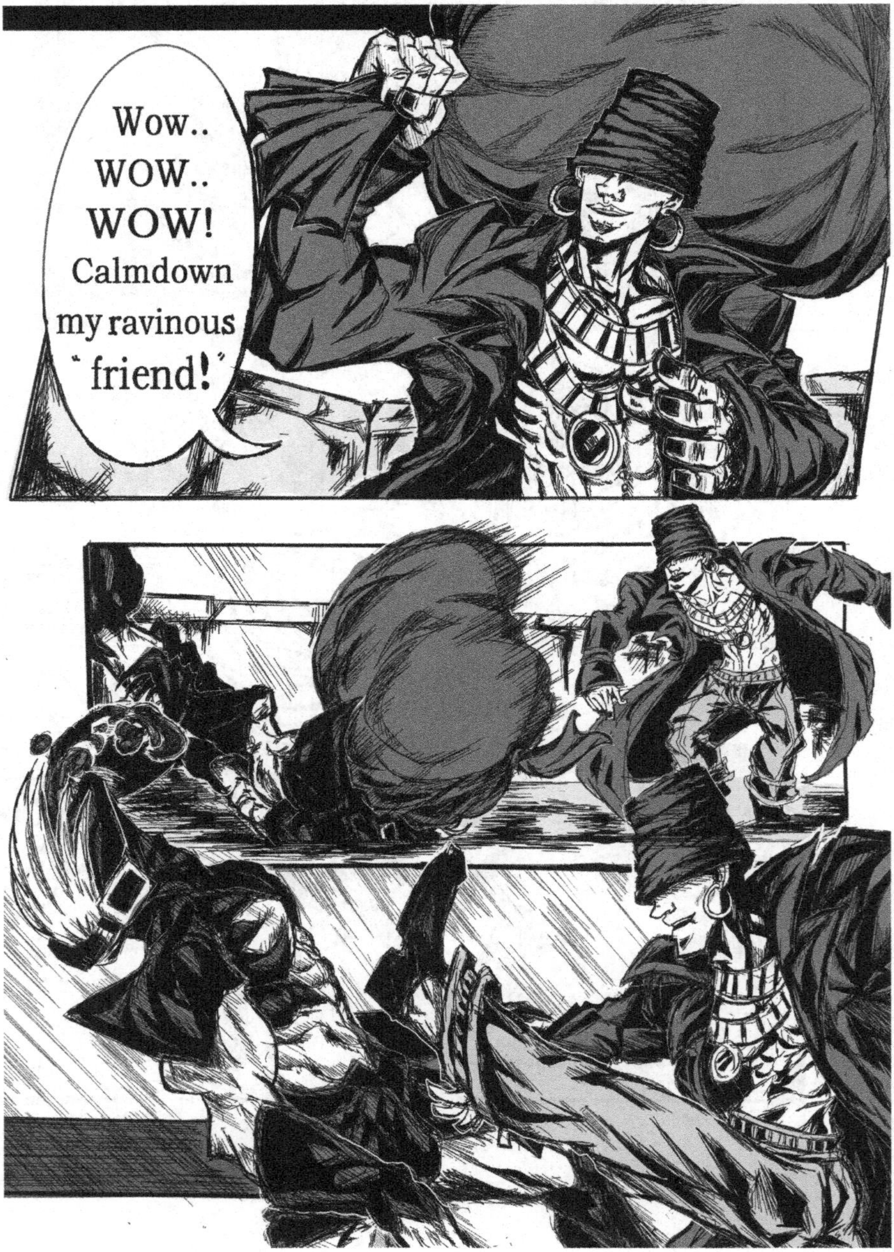
Wow.. WOW.. WOW! Calmdown my ravinous "friend!"

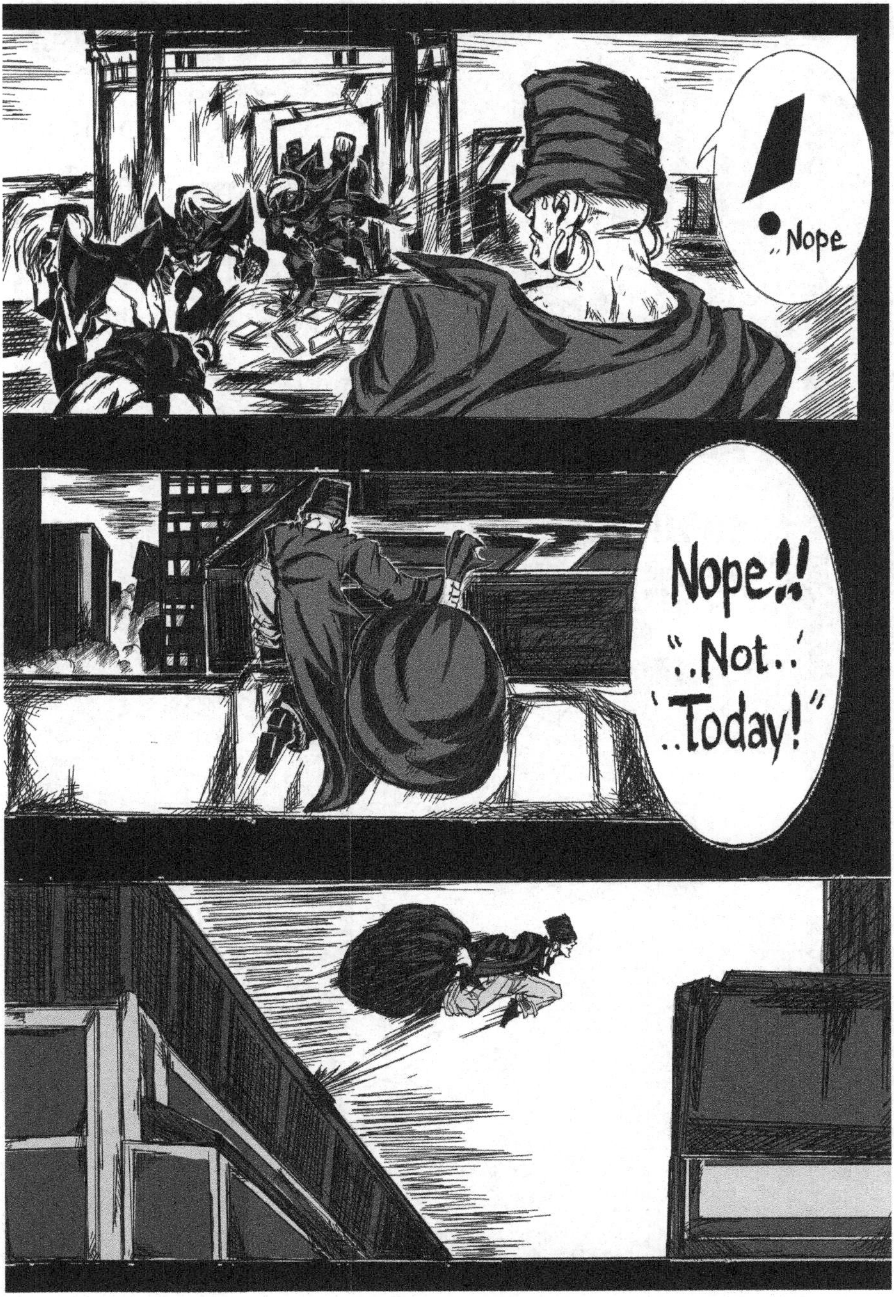
!
..Nope
Nope!!
"..Not..
..Today!"

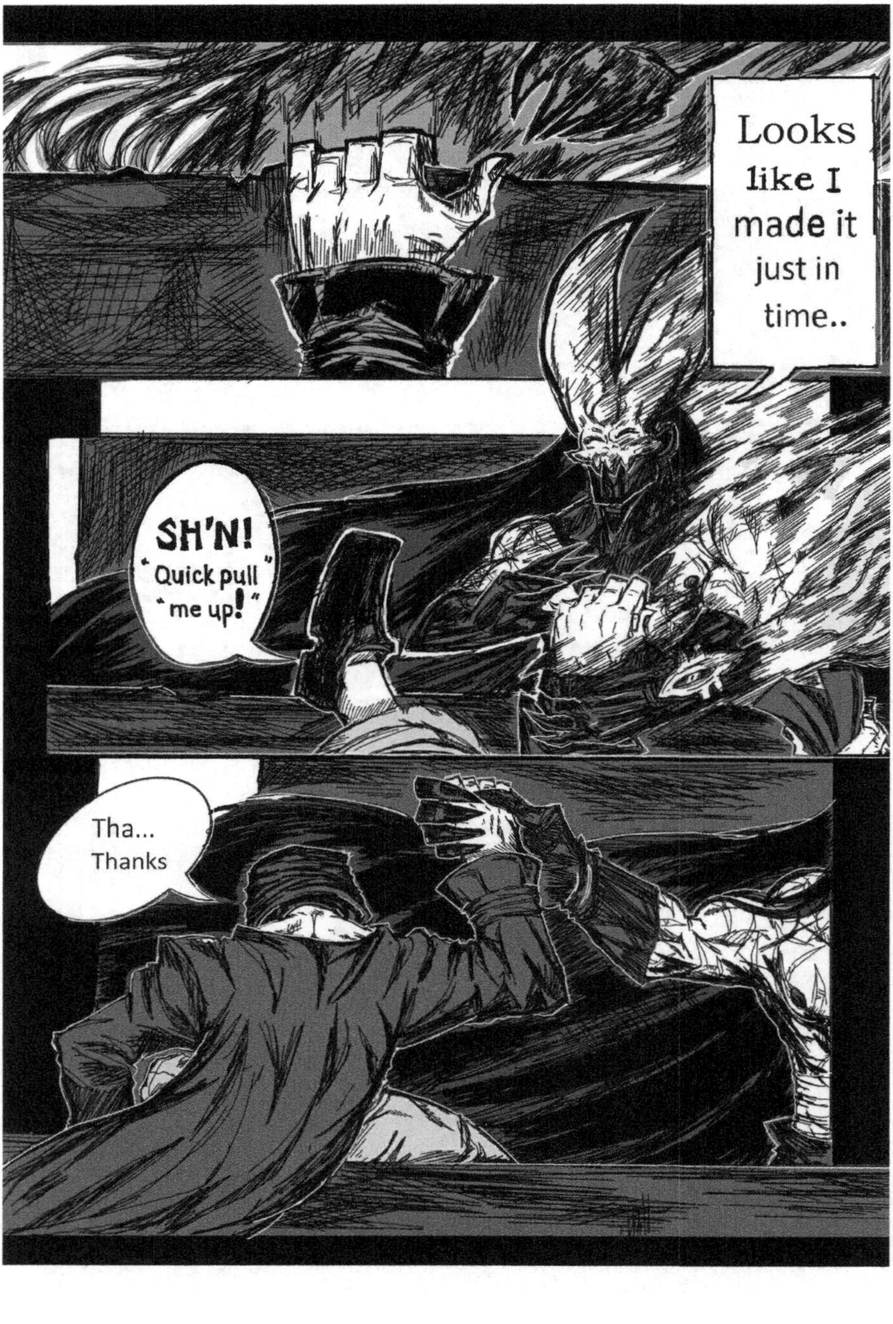
Looks like I made it just in time..
SH'N!
"Quick pull me up!"
Tha... Thanks

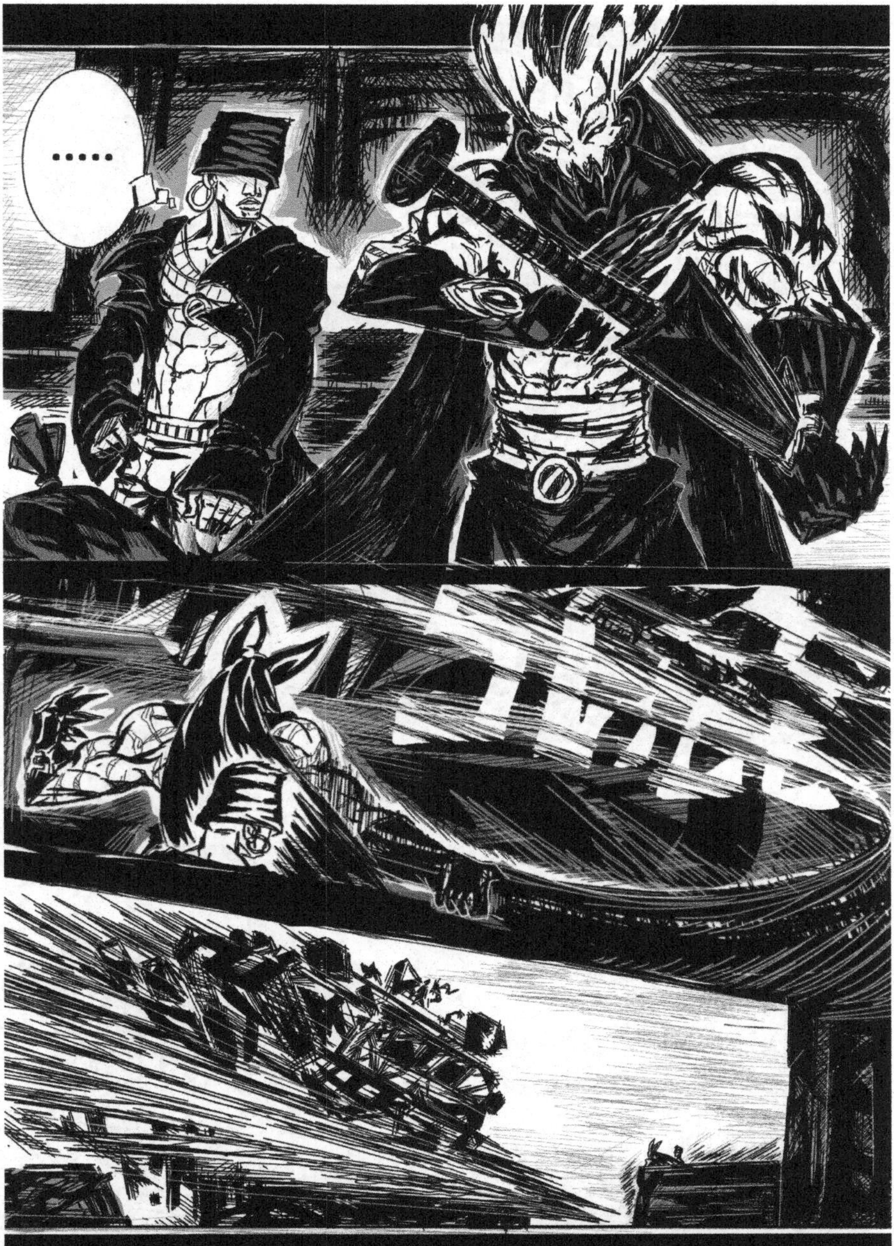

.....

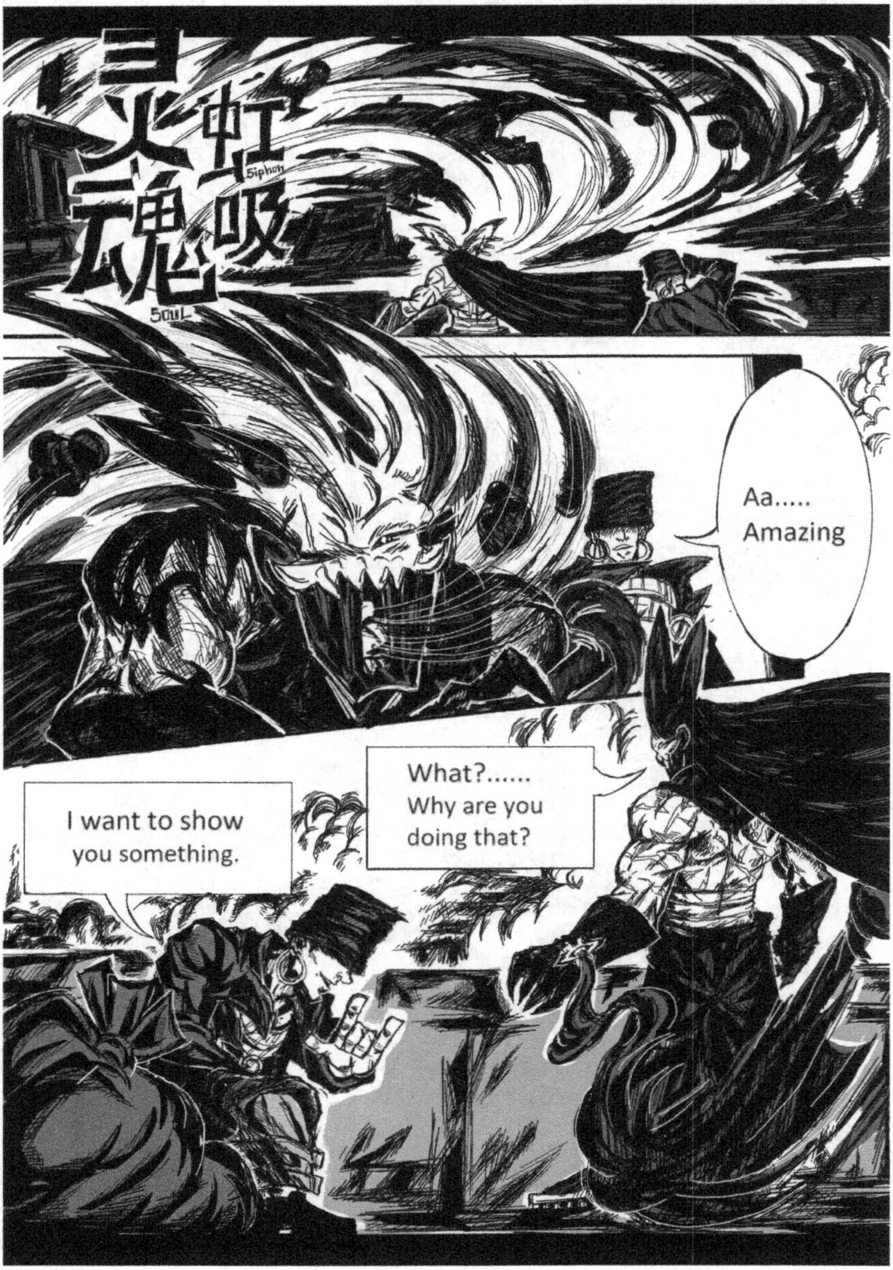

灵魂虹吸
Soul
Siphon
Aa.....
Amazing
What?......
Why are you
doing that?
I want to show
you something.

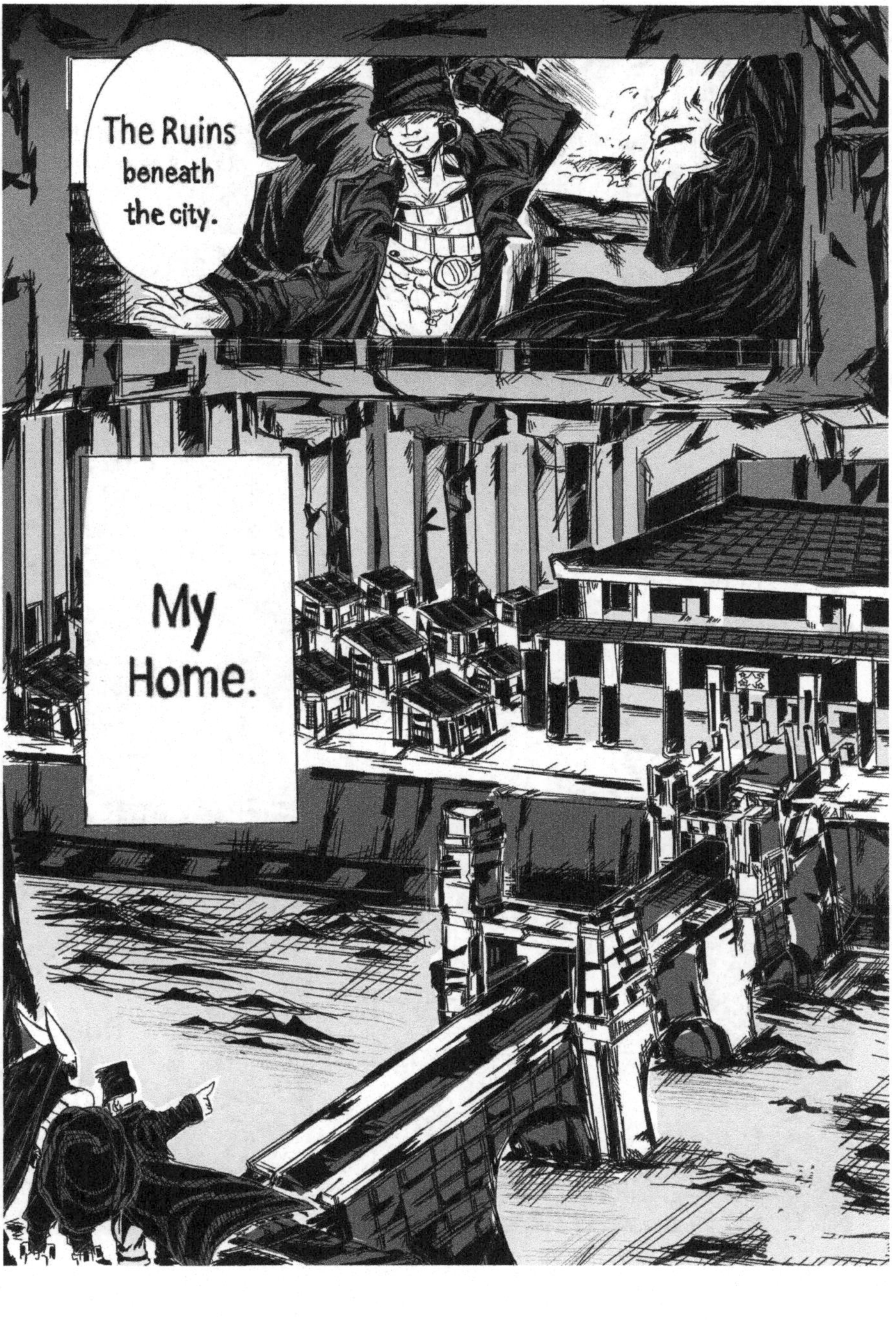
The Ruins beneath the city.
My Home.

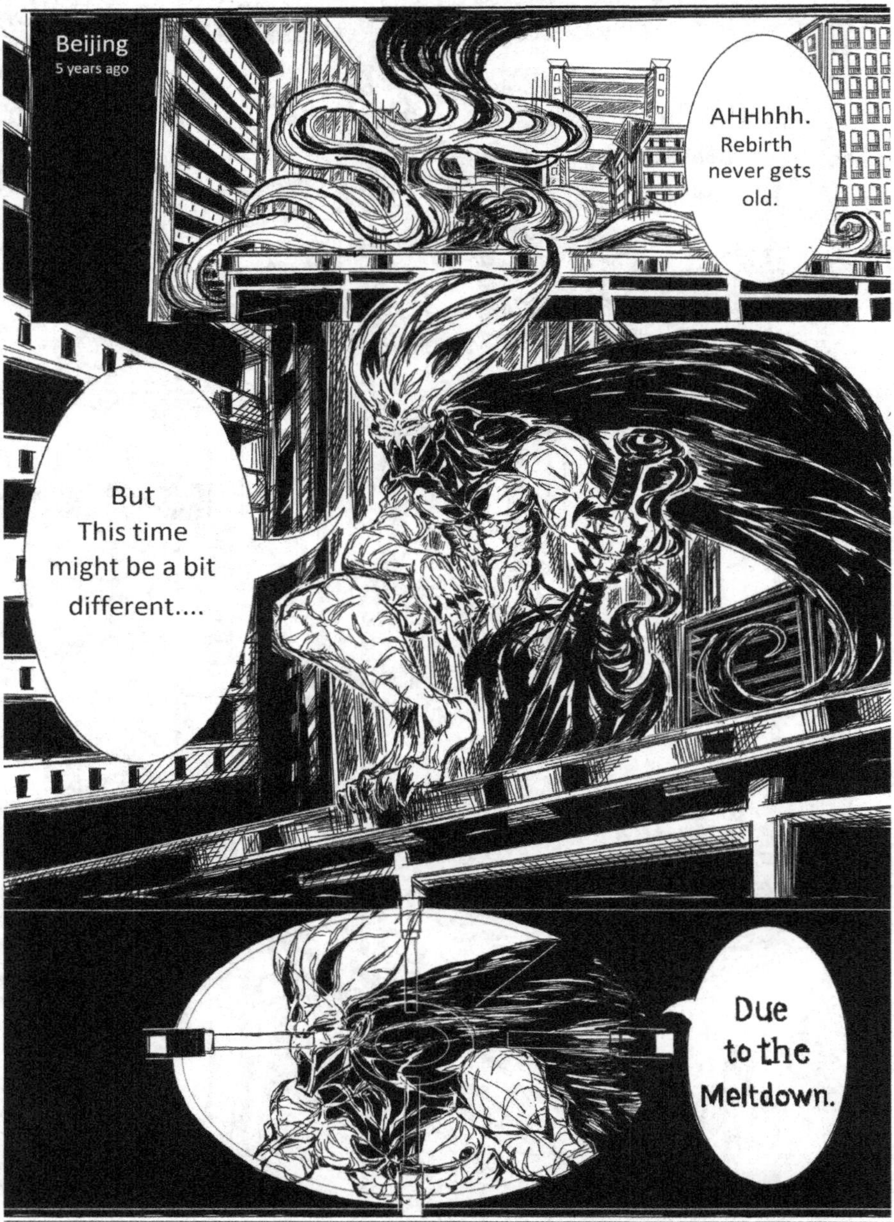
Beijing
5 years ago
AHHhhh. Rebirth never gets old.
But This time might be a bit different....
Due to the Meltdown.

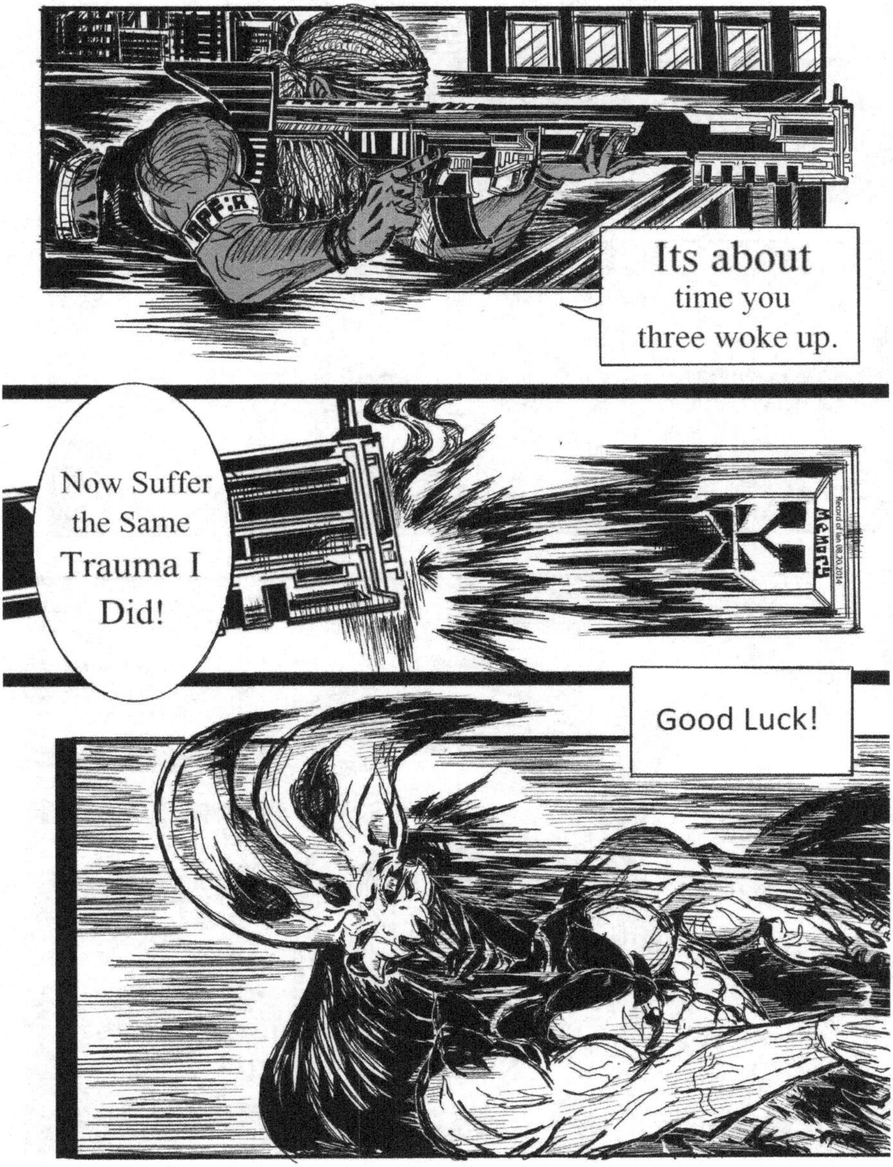
Its about time you three woke up.
Now Suffer the Same Trauma I Did!
Record of Ian 08.20.2014
Good Luck!

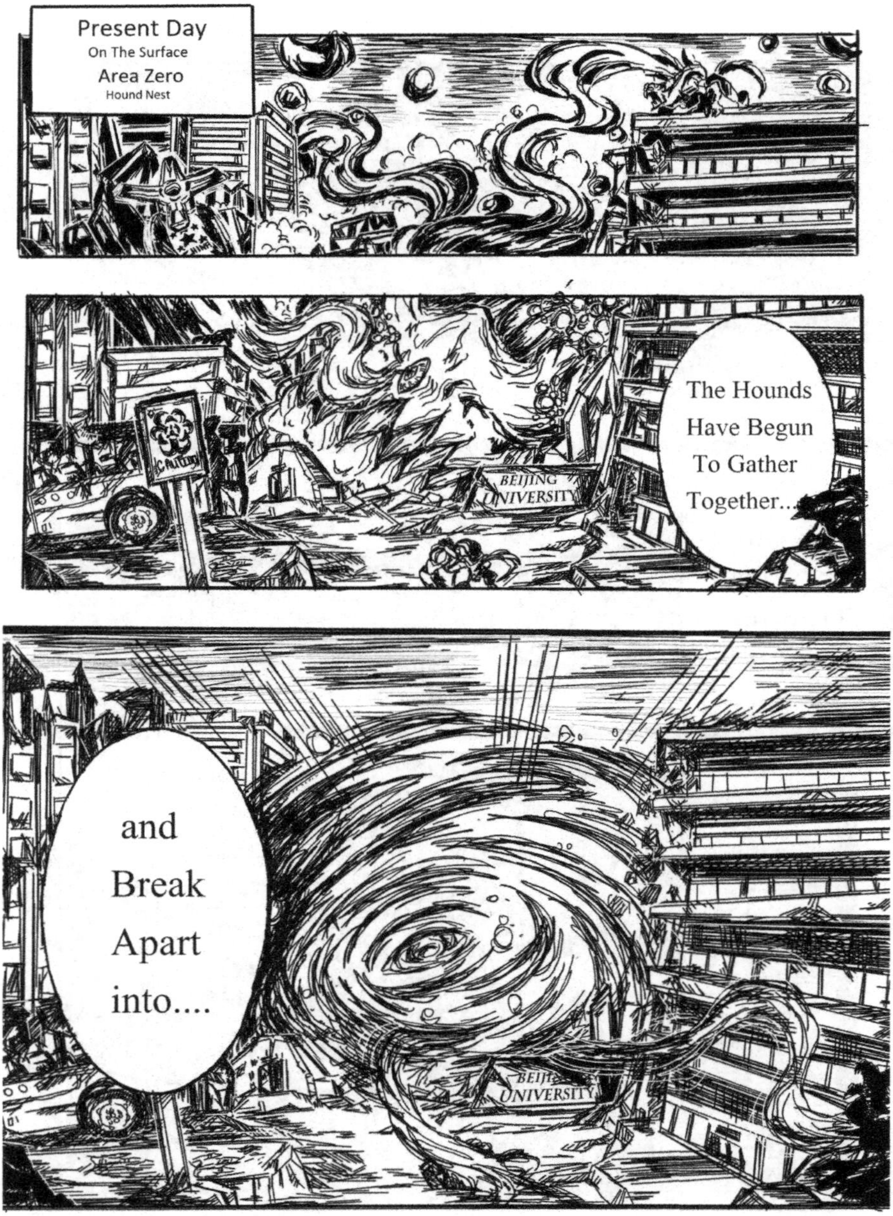
Present Day
On The Surface
Area Zero
Hound Nest
CAUTION
BEIJING UNIVERSITY
The Hounds Have Begun To Gather Together...
and Break Apart into....
BEIJING UNIVERSITY

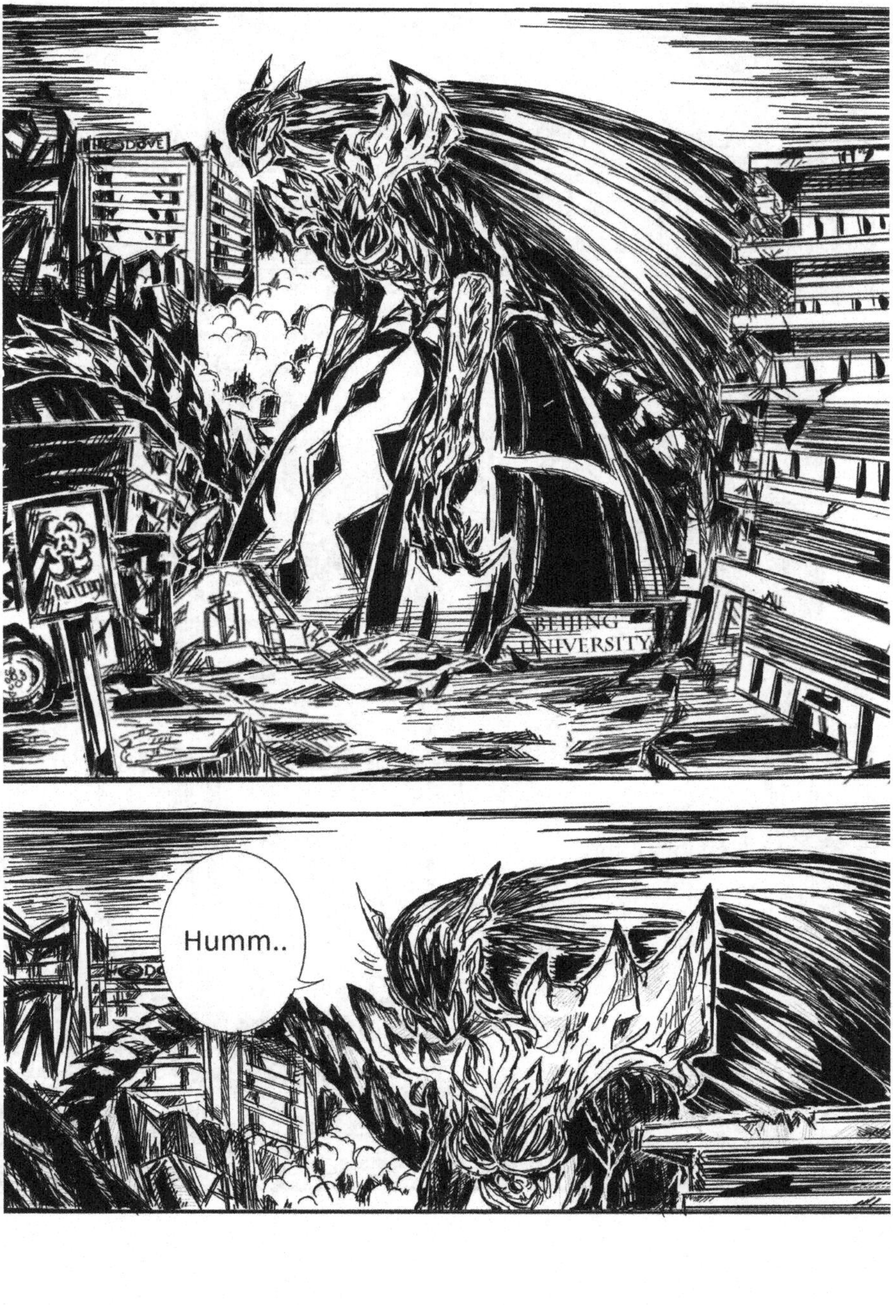
DOVE
BEIJING
UNIVERSITY
Humm..

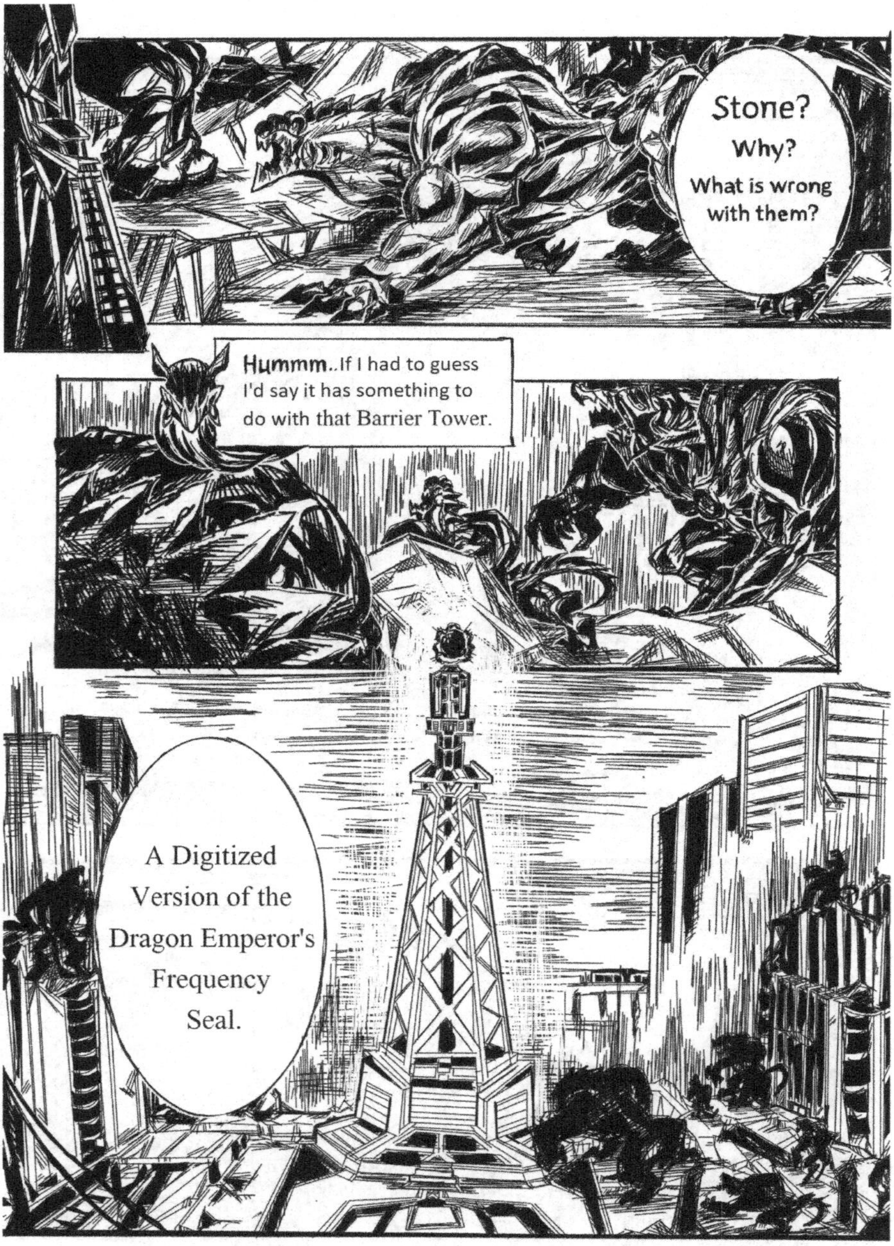
Stone?
Why?
What is wrong with them?
Hummmm..If I had to guess I'd say it has something to do with that Barrier Tower.
A Digitized Version of the Dragon Emperor's Frequency Seal.

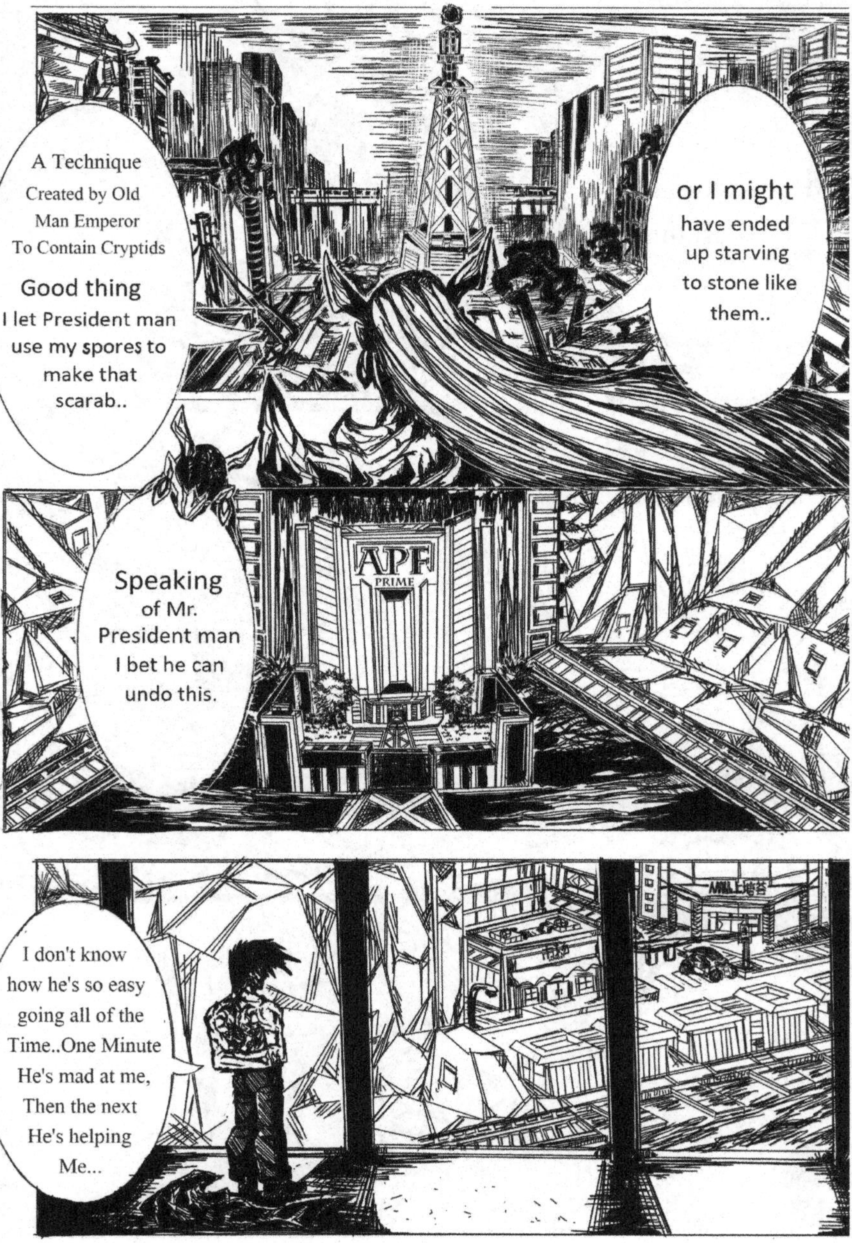
A Technique Created by Old Man Emperor To Contain Cryptids
Good thing I let President man use my spores to make that scarab..
or I might have ended up starving to stone like them..
APF PRIME
Speaking of Mr. President man I bet he can undo this.
I don't know how he's so easy going all of the Time..One Minute He's mad at me, Then the next He's helping Me...

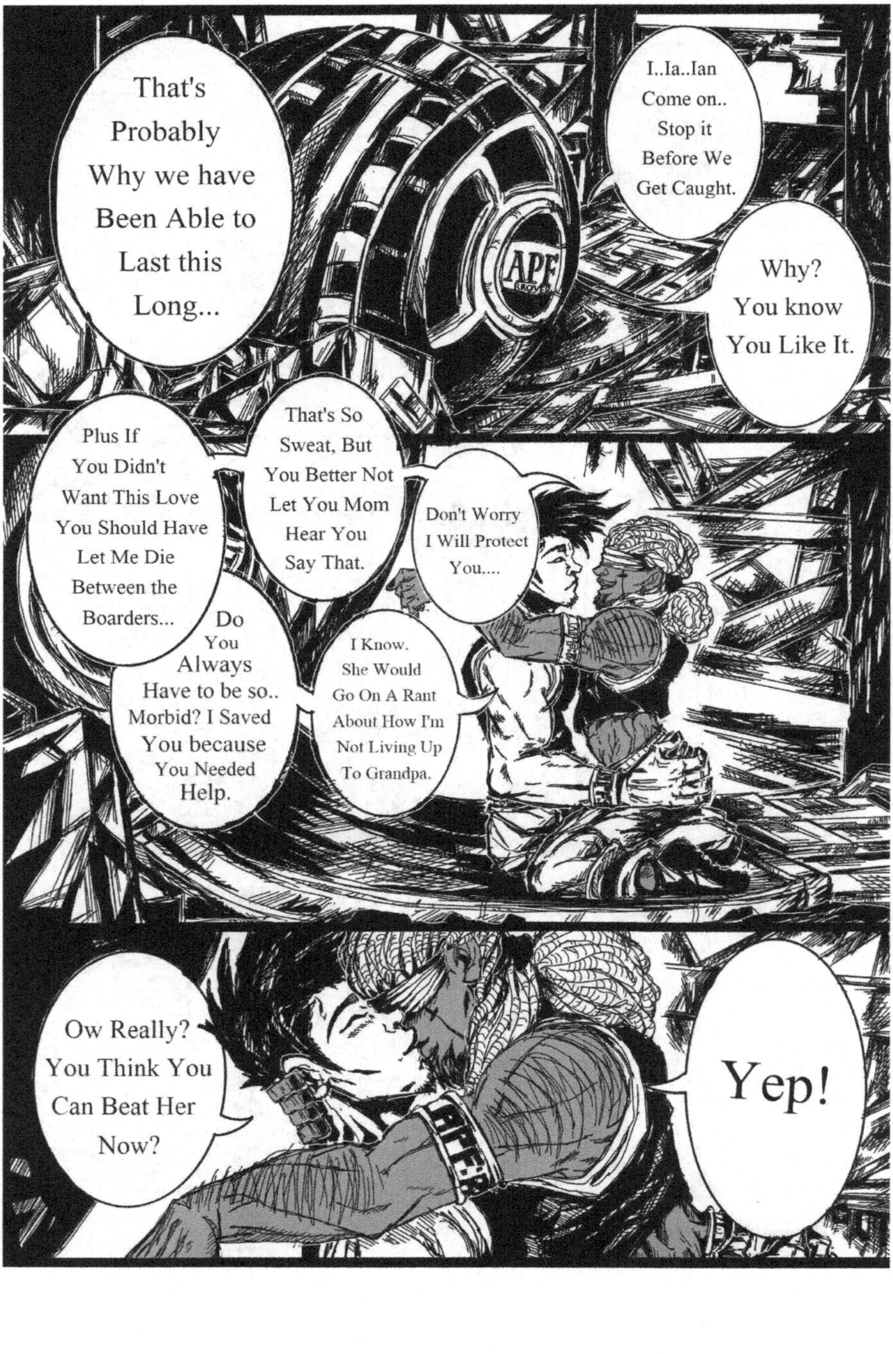
That's Probably Why we have Been Able to Last this Long...
I..Ia..Ian Come on.. Stop it Before We Get Caught.
Why? You know You Like It.
APF
Plus If You Didn't Want This Love You Should Have Let Me Die Between the Boarders...
That's So Sweat, But You Better Not Let You Mom Hear You Say That.
Don't Worry I Will Protect You....
Do You Always Have to be so.. Morbid? I Saved You because You Needed Help.
I Know. She Would Go On A Rant About How I'm Not Living Up To Grandpa.
Ow Really? You Think You Can Beat Her Now?
Yep!

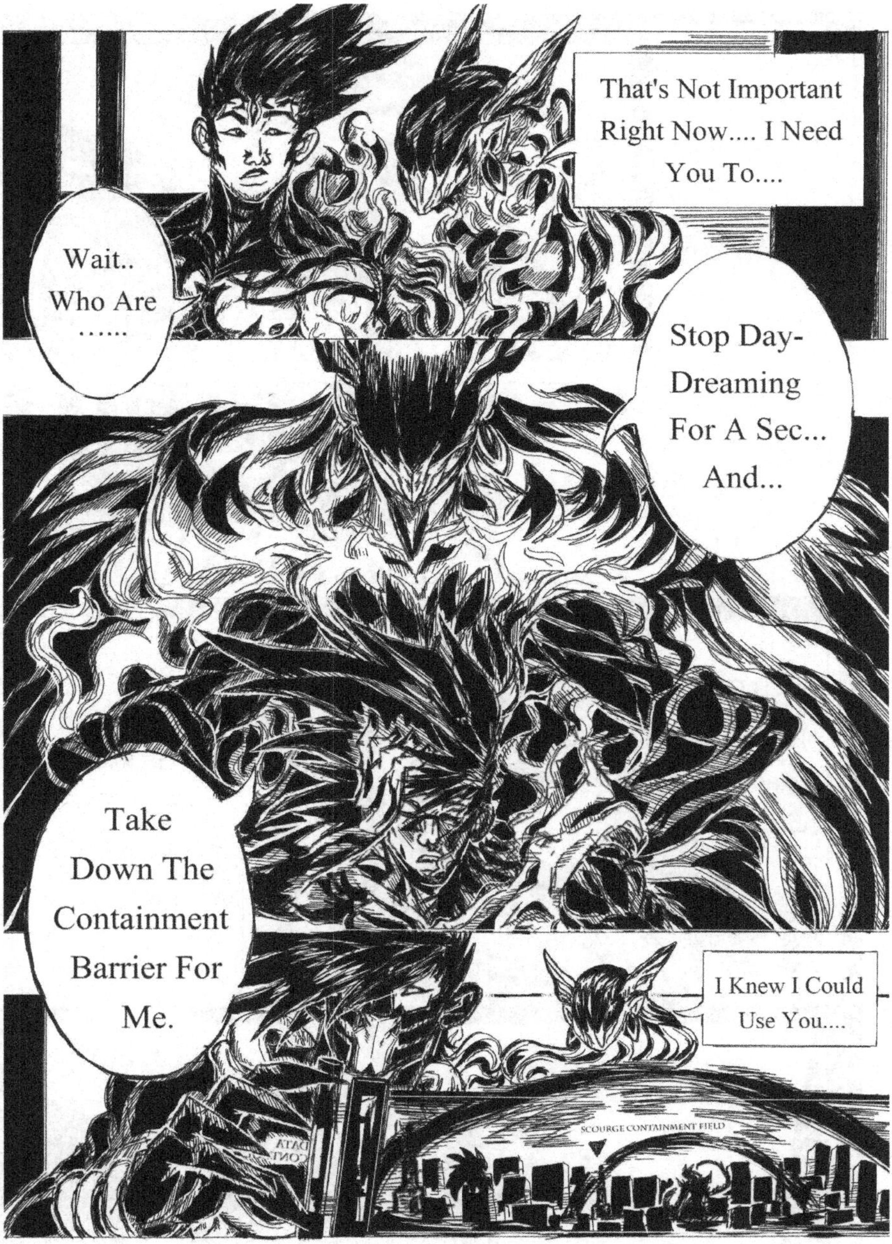
Wait.. Who Are ……
That's Not Important Right Now.... I Need You To....
Stop Day-Dreaming For A Sec... And...
Take Down The Containment Barrier For Me.
I Knew I Could Use You....
SCOURGE CONTAINMENT FIELD

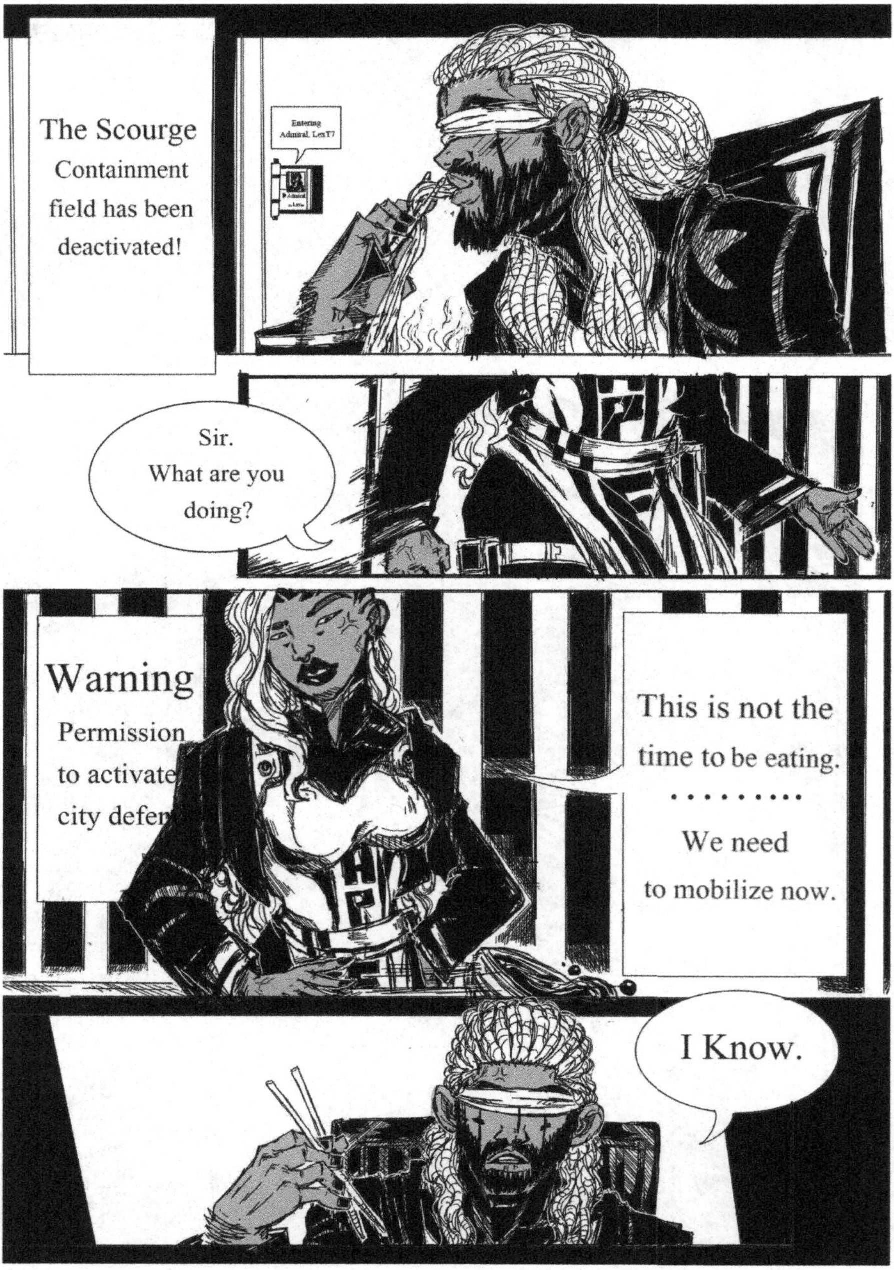
The Scourge Containment field has been deactivated!
Entering Admiral. LexT7
Sir. What are you doing?
Warning Permission to activate city defen
This is not the time to be eating. .... We need to mobilize now.
I Know.

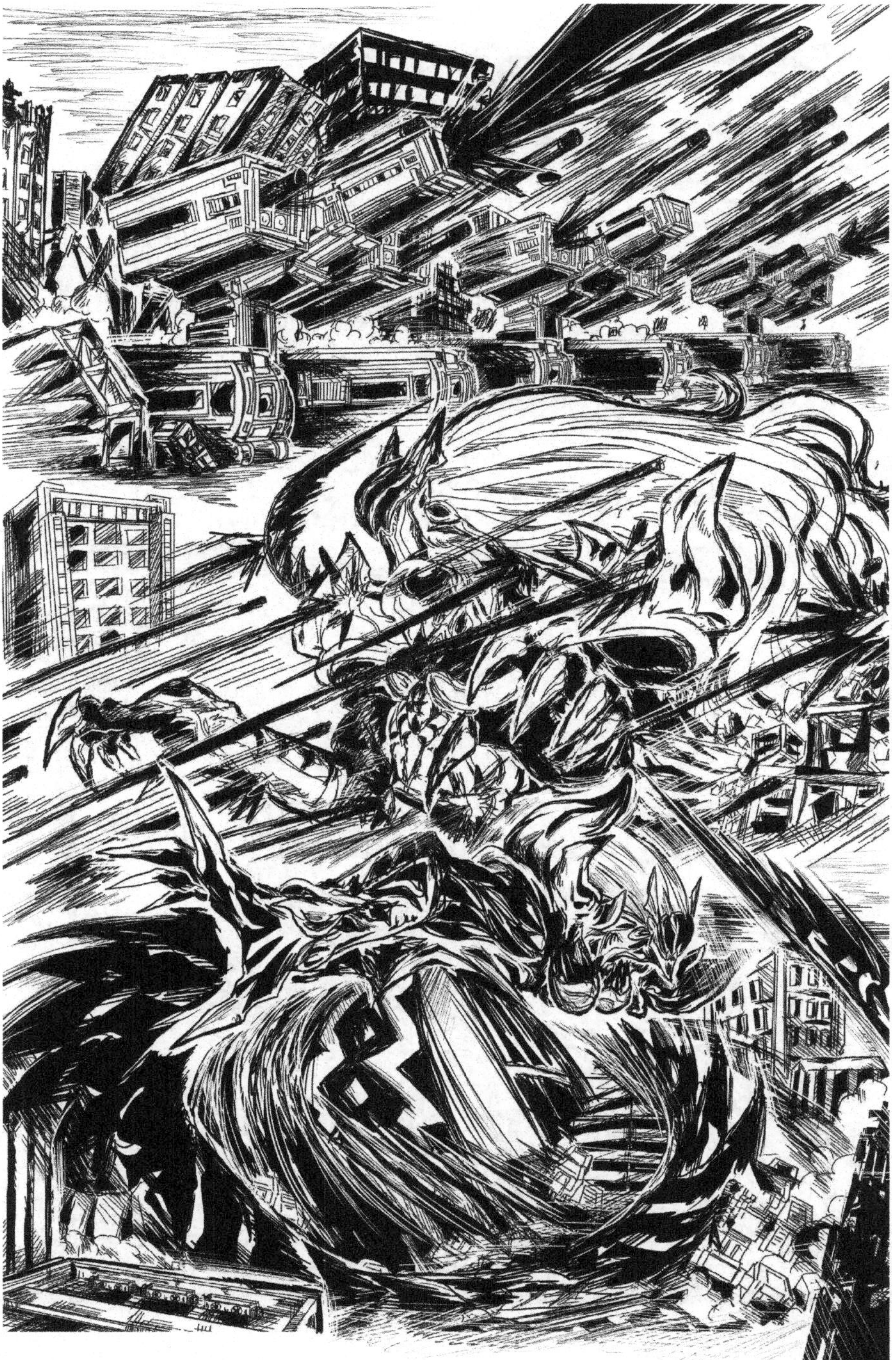

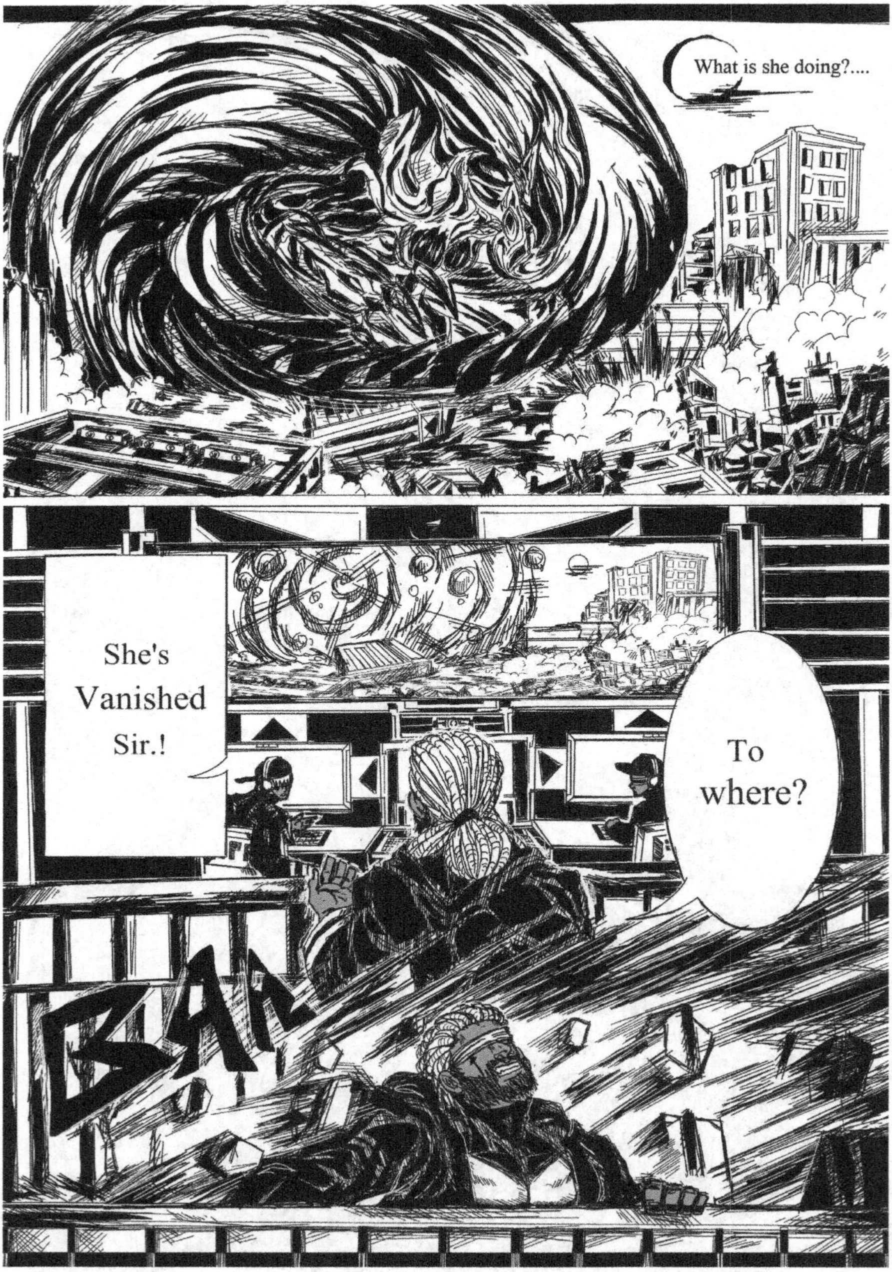
What is she doing?....
She's Vanished Sir.!
To where?

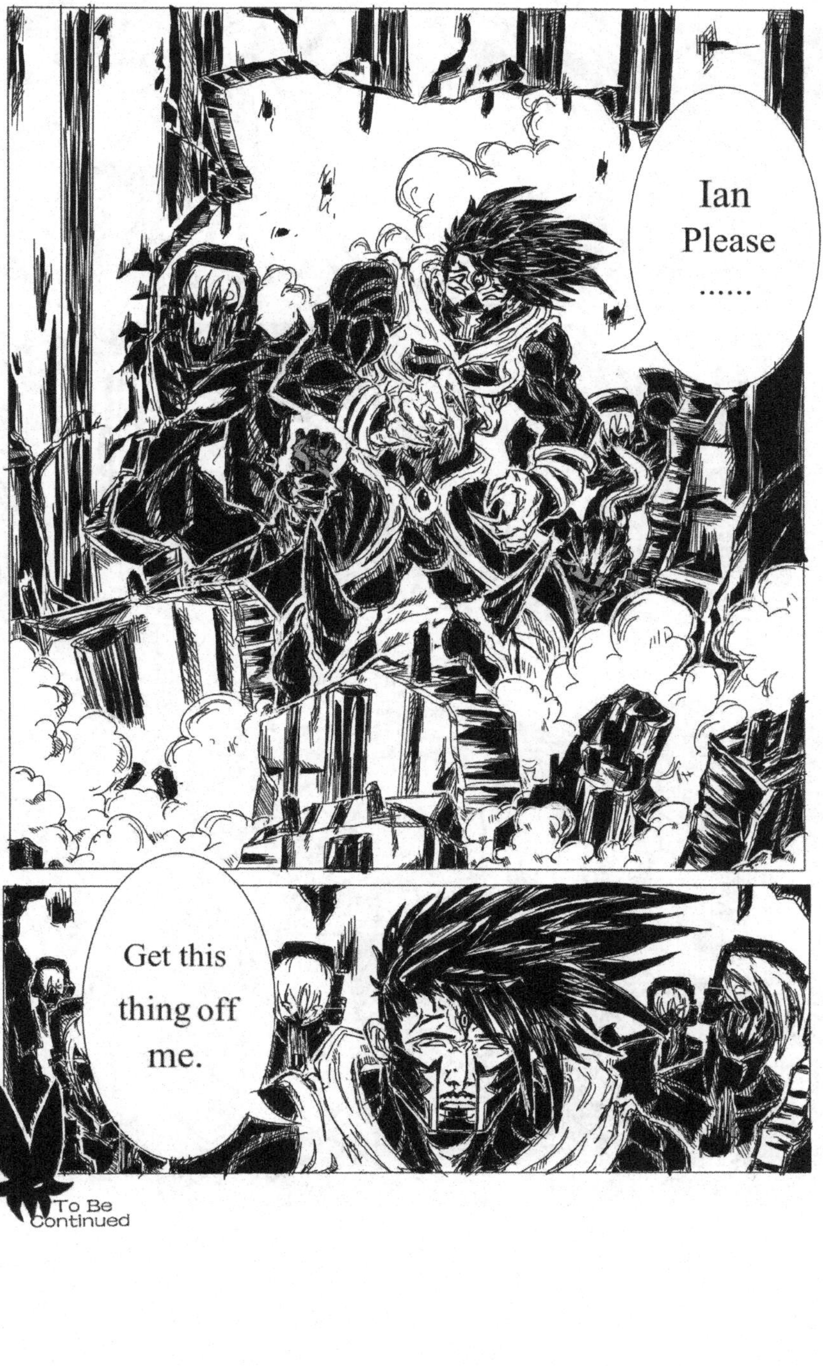
Ian
Please
......
Get this
thing off
me.

To Be
Continued

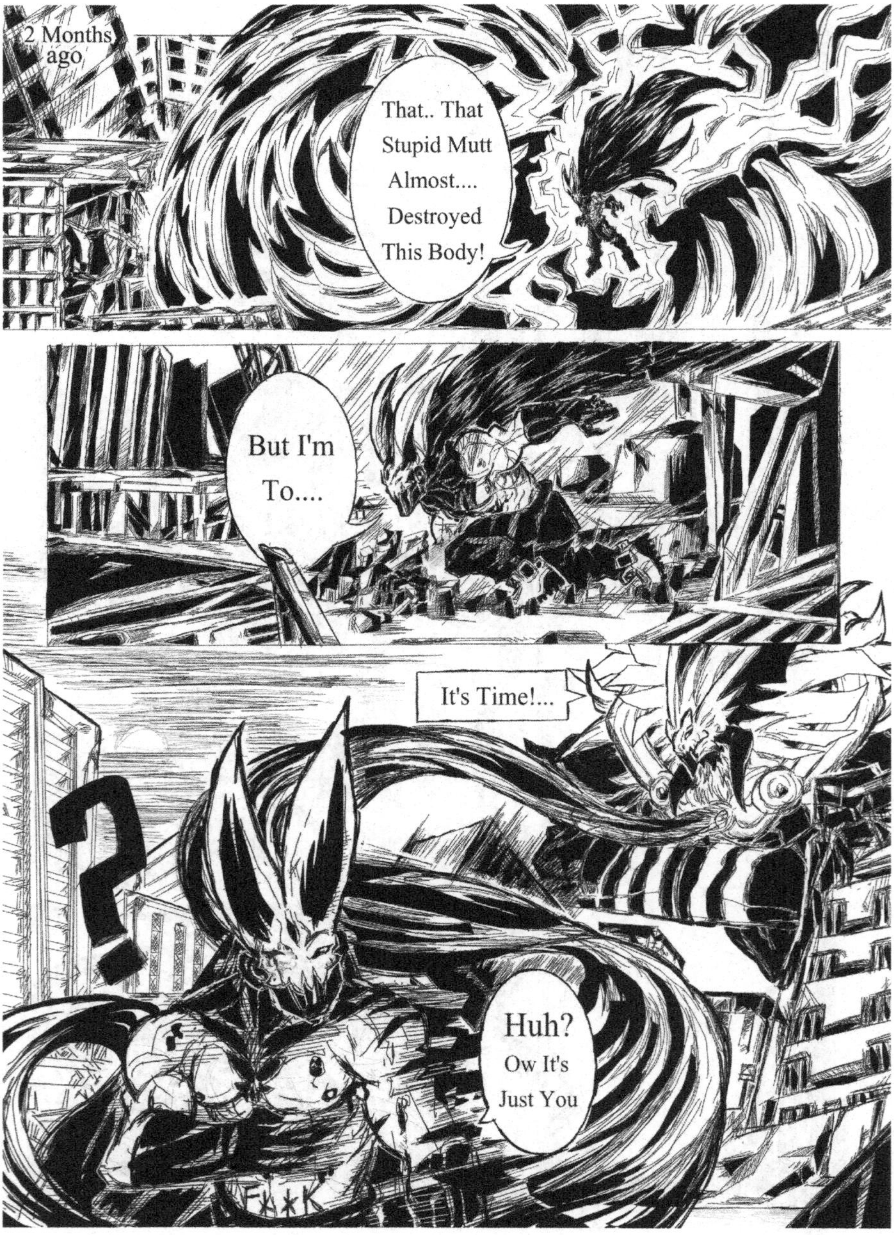
2 Months ago
That.. That Stupid Mutt Almost.... Destroyed This Body!
But I'm To....
It's Time!...
?
Huh? Ow It's Just You
F**K

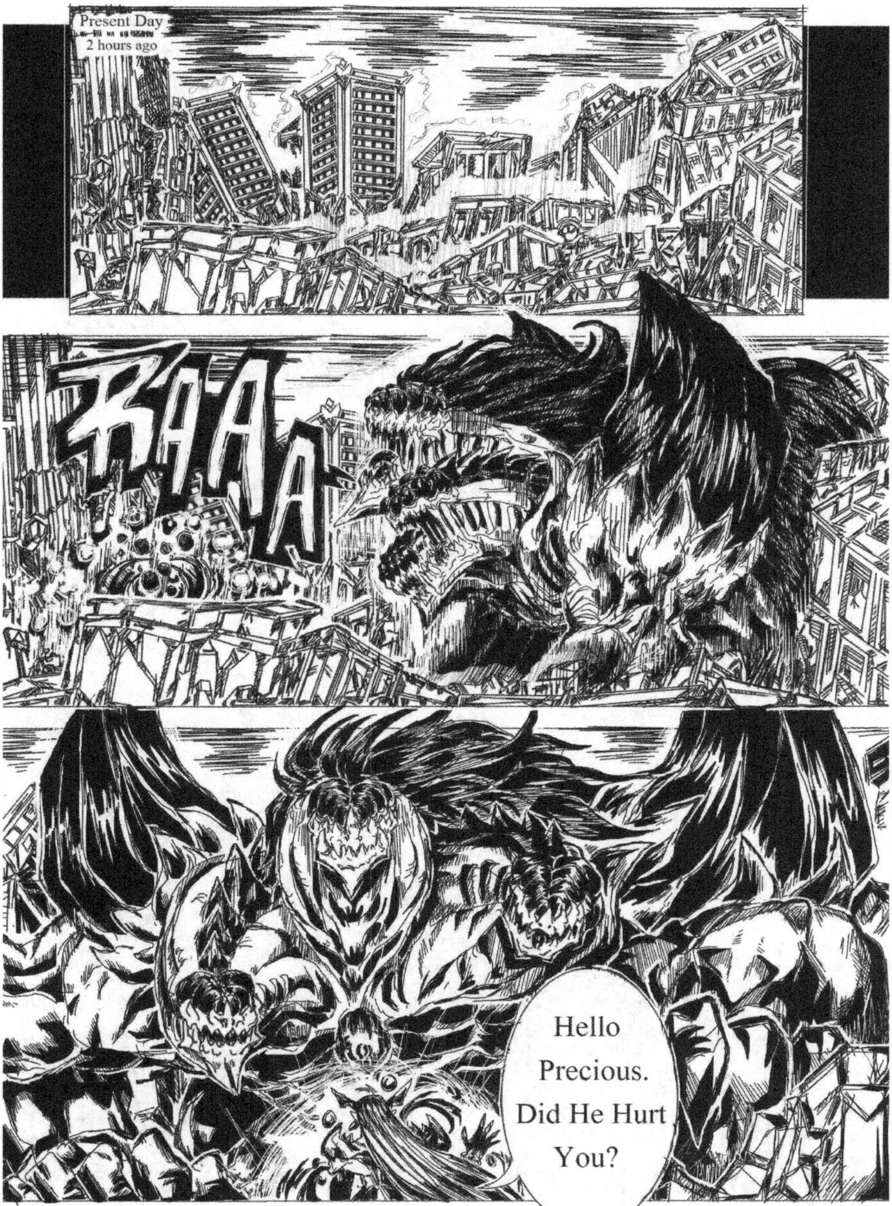
Present Day
2 hours ago
RAAA
Hello Precious. Did He Hurt You?

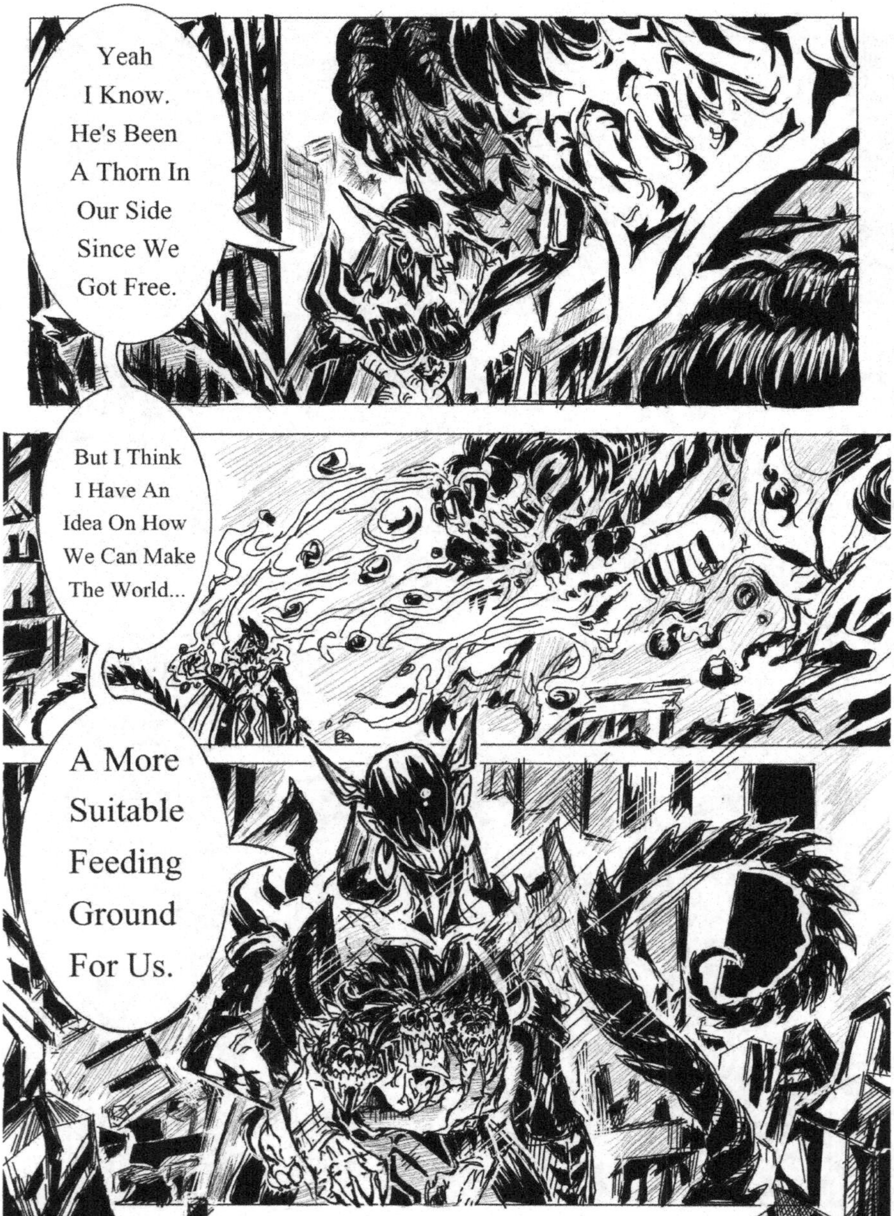
Yeah I Know. He's Been A Thorn In Our Side Since We Got Free.
But I Think I Have An Idea On How We Can Make The World...
A More Suitable Feeding Ground For Us.

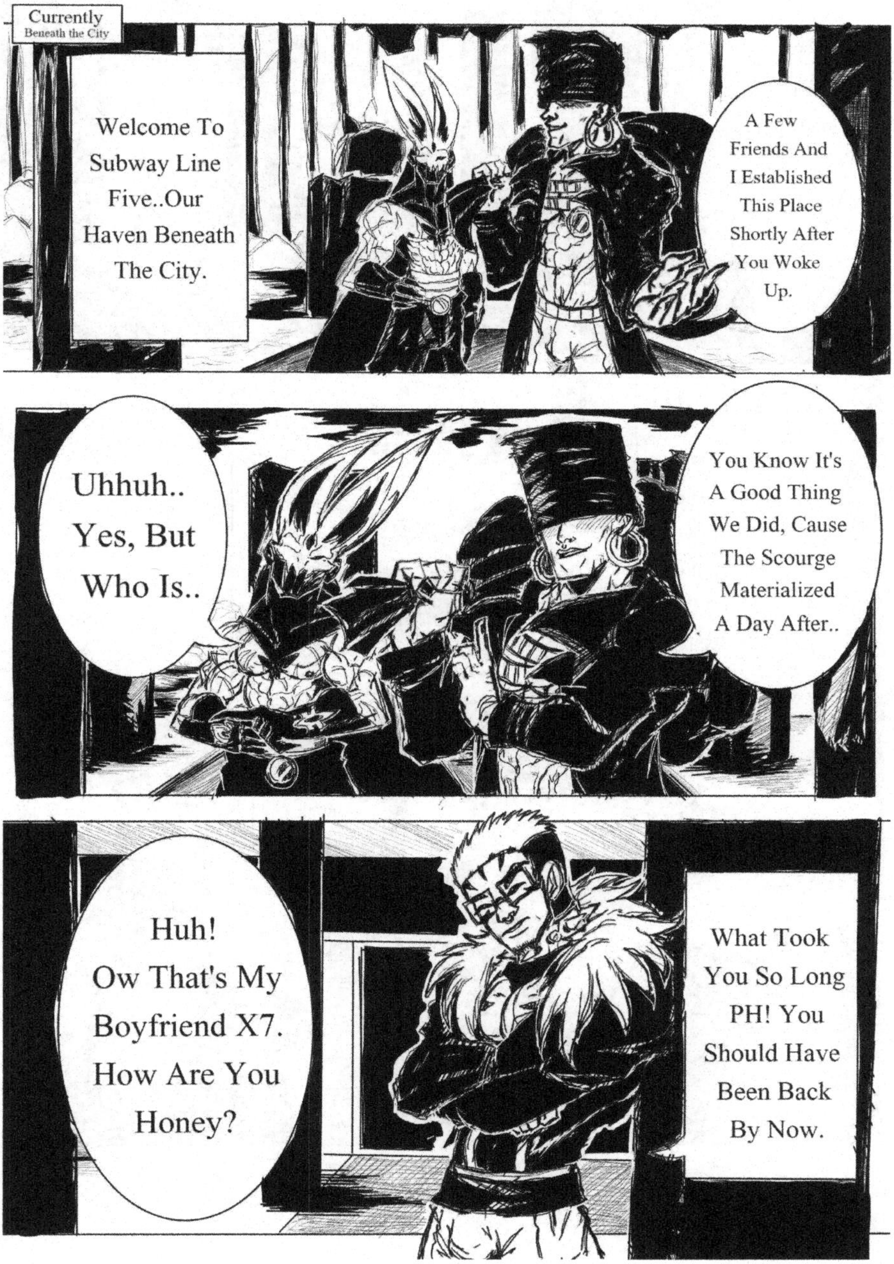
Currently
Beneath the City
Welcome To Subway Line Five..Our Haven Beneath The City.
A Few Friends And I Established This Place Shortly After You Woke Up.
Uhhuh.. Yes, But Who Is..
You Know It's A Good Thing We Did, Cause The Scourge Materialized A Day After..
Huh! Ow That's My Boyfriend X7. How Are You Honey?
What Took You So Long PH! You Should Have Been Back By Now.

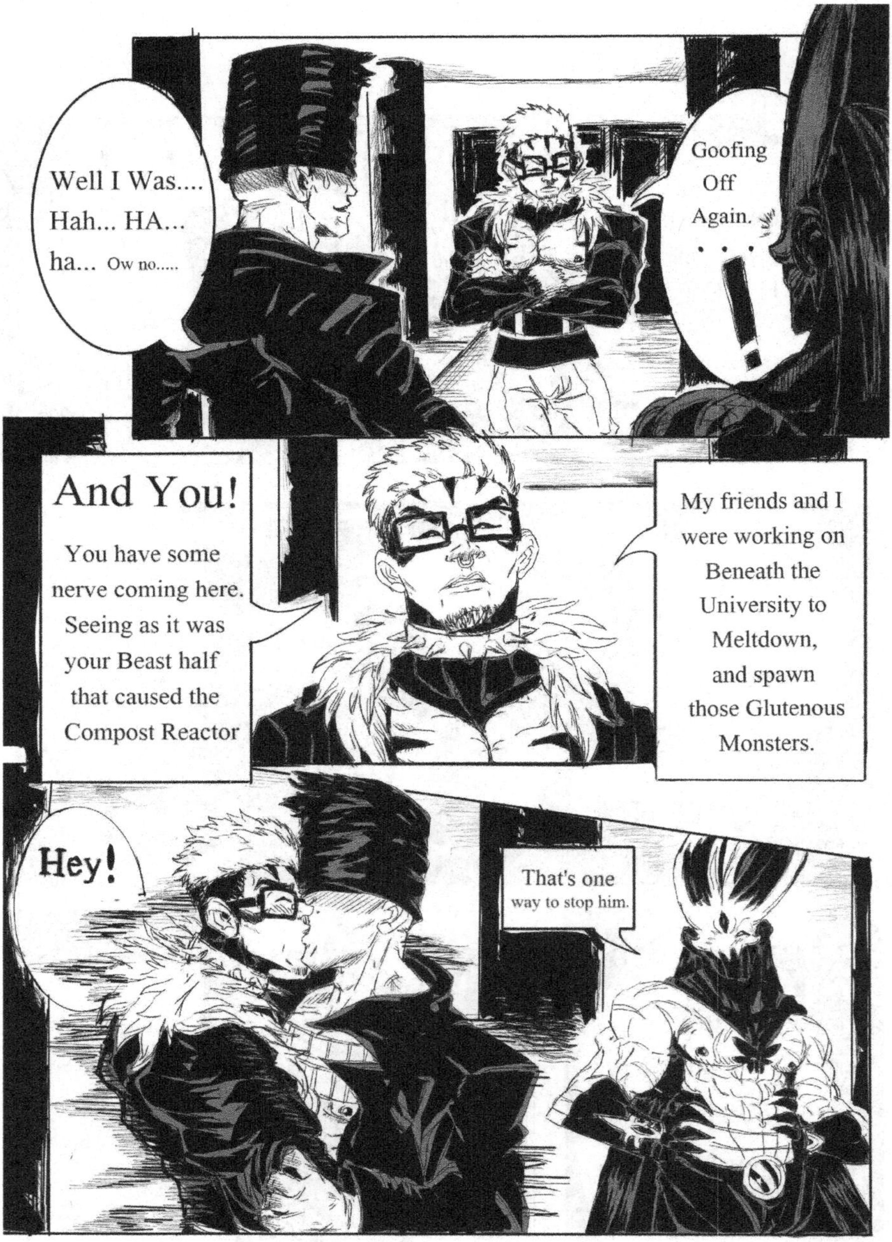
Well I Was.... Hah... HA... ha... Ow no.....
Goofing Off Again.
. . .
!
And You!
You have some nerve coming here. Seeing as it was your Beast half that caused the Compost Reactor
My friends and I were working on Beneath the University to Meltdown, and spawn those Glutenous Monsters.
Hey!
That's one way to stop him.

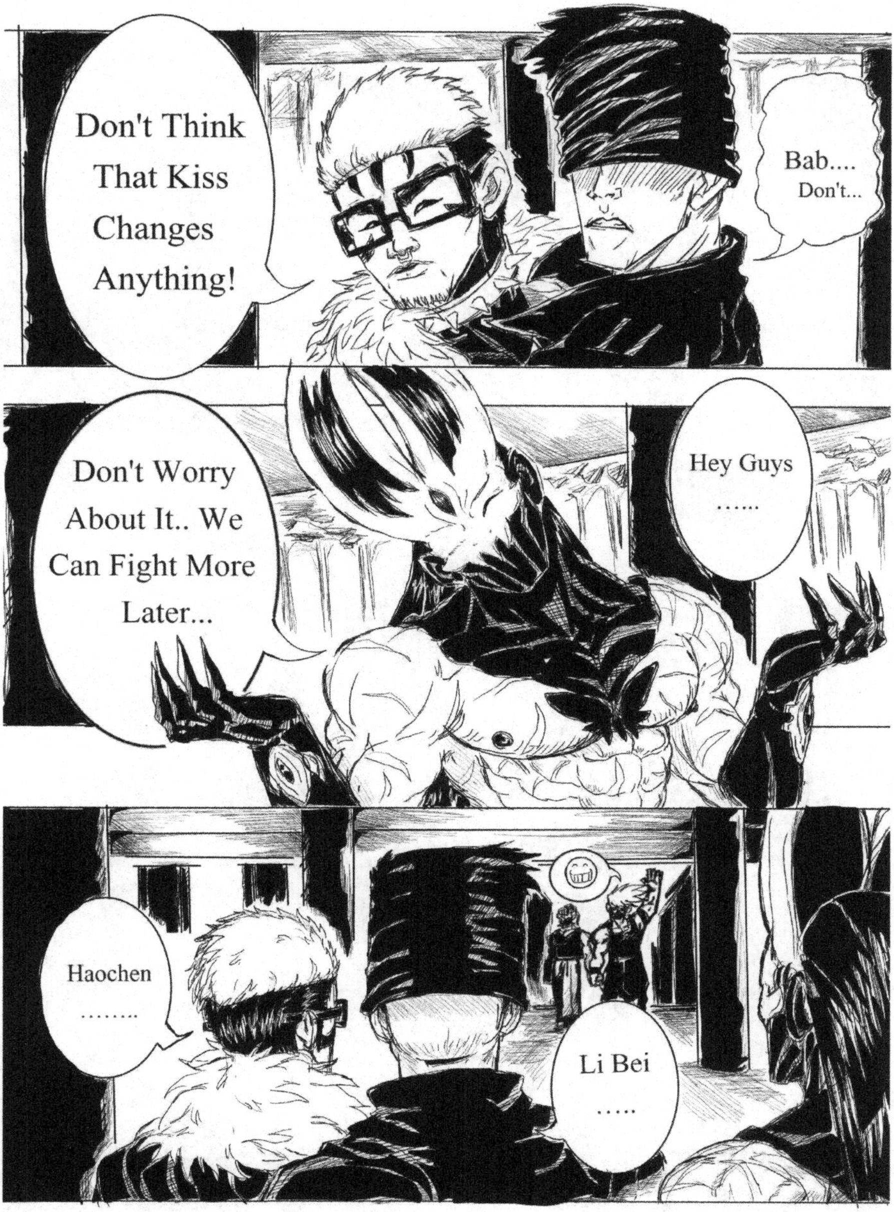
Don't Think That Kiss Changes Anything!
Bab.... Don't...
Don't Worry About It.. We Can Fight More Later...
Hey Guys ......
Haochen ....
Li Bei .....

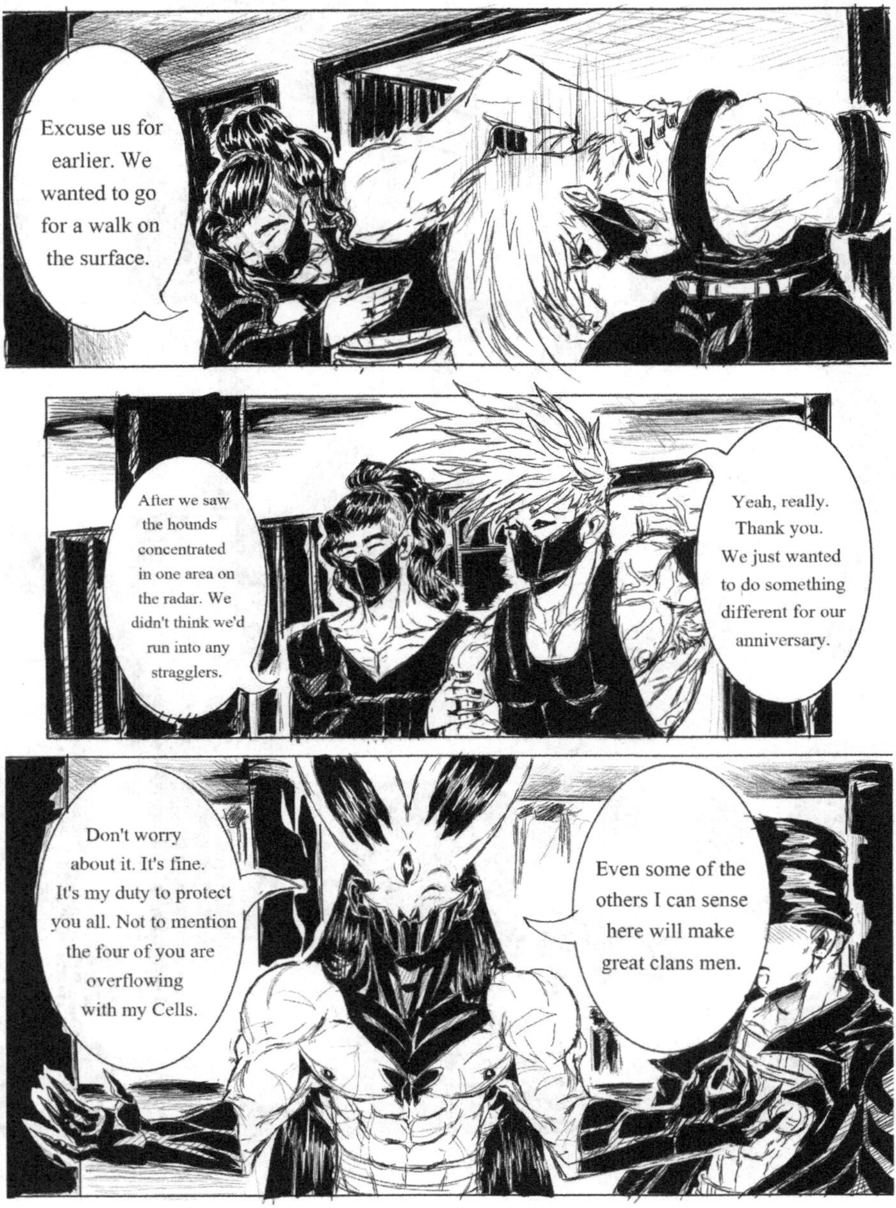
Excuse us for earlier. We wanted to go for a walk on the surface.
After we saw the hounds concentrated in one area on the radar. We didn't think we'd run into any stragglers.
Yeah, really. Thank you. We just wanted to do something different for our anniversary.
Don't worry about it. It's fine. It's my duty to protect you all. Not to mention the four of you are overflowing with my Cells.
Even some of the others I can sense here will make great clans men.

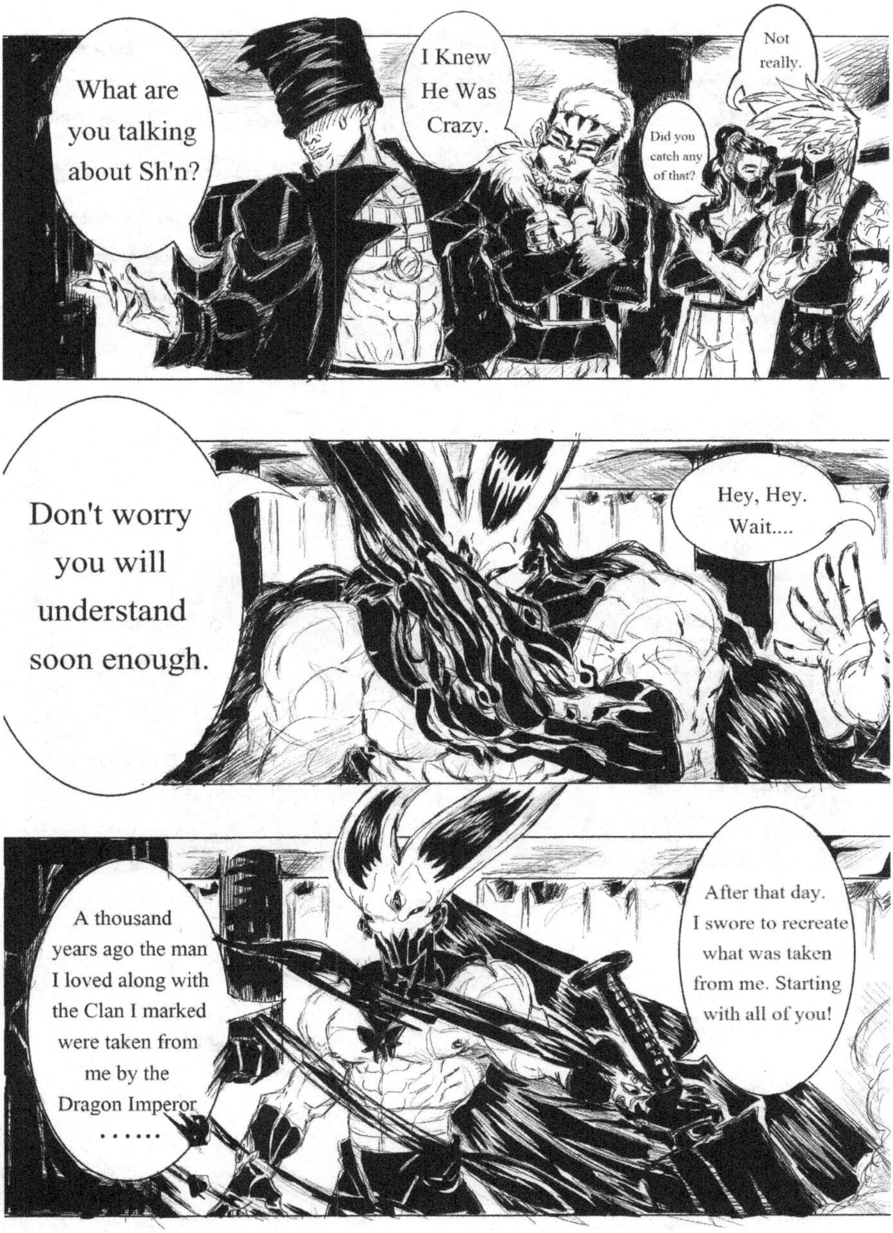
What are you talking about Sh'n?
I Knew He Was Crazy.
Not really.
Did you catch any of that?
Don't worry you will understand soon enough.
Hey, Hey. Wait....
A thousand years ago the man I loved along with the Clan I marked were taken from me by the Dragon Imperor ......
After that day. I swore to recreate what was taken from me. Starting with all of you!

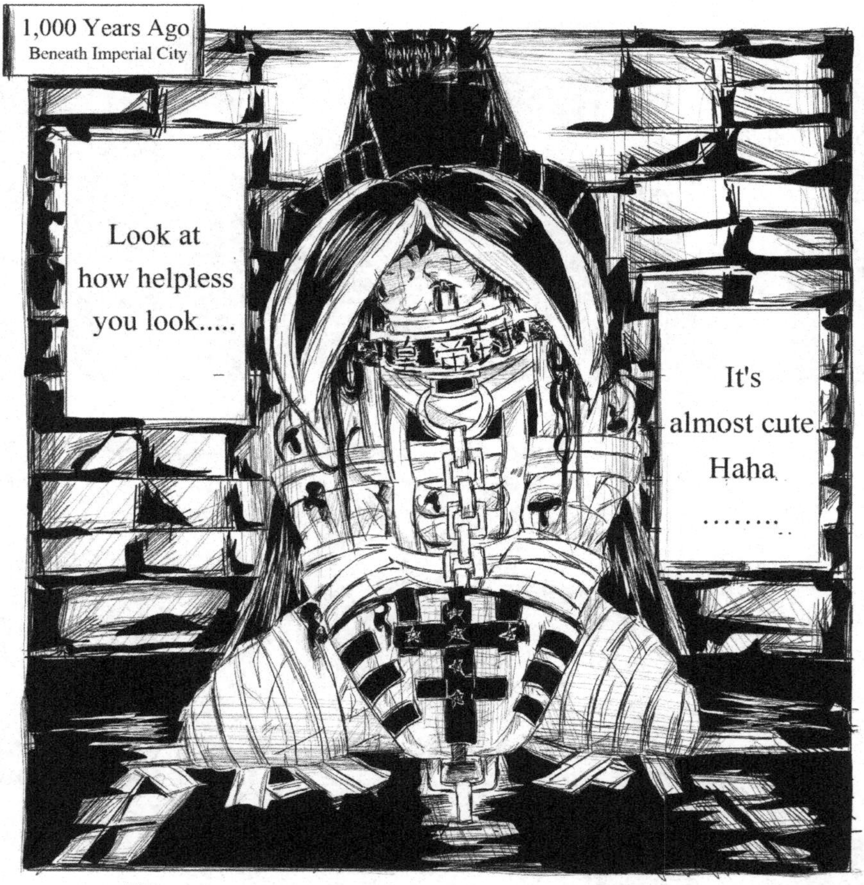
1,000 Years Ago
Beneath Imperial City
Look at how helpless you look.....
It's almost cute. Haha ....

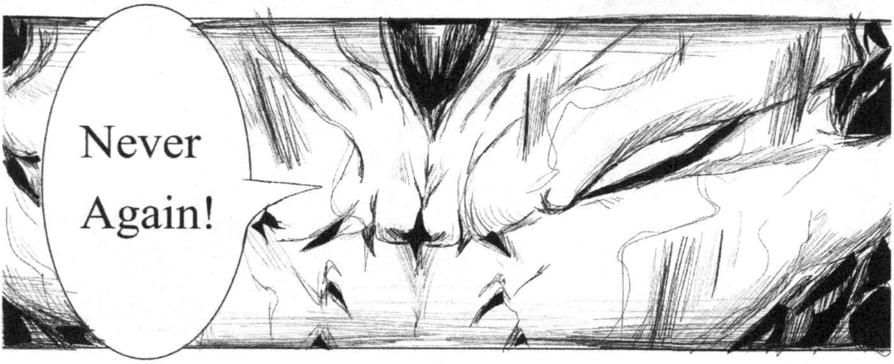
Never Again!

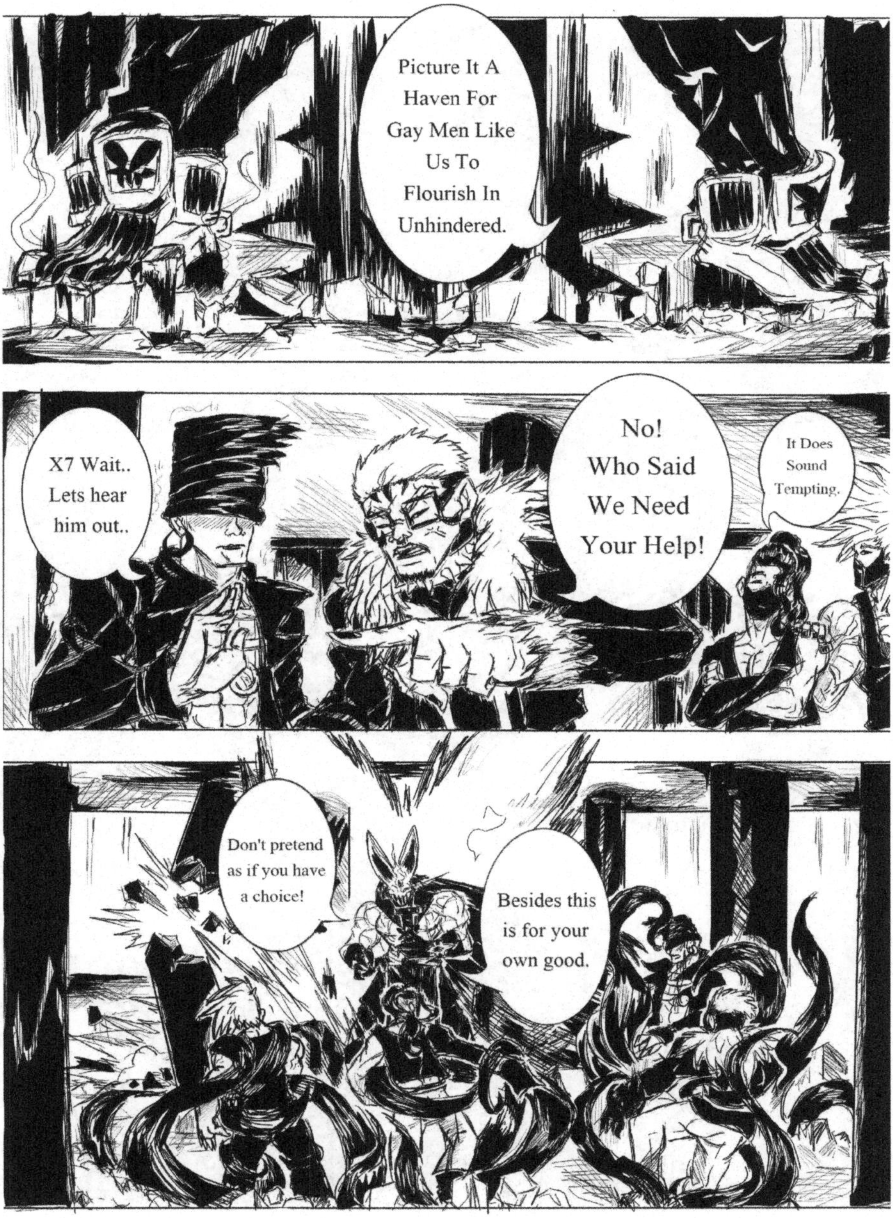
Picture It A Haven For Gay Men Like Us To Flourish In Unhindered.
X7 Wait.. Lets hear him out..
No! Who Said We Need Your Help!
It Does Sound Tempting.
Don't pretend as if you have a choice!
Besides this is for your own good.

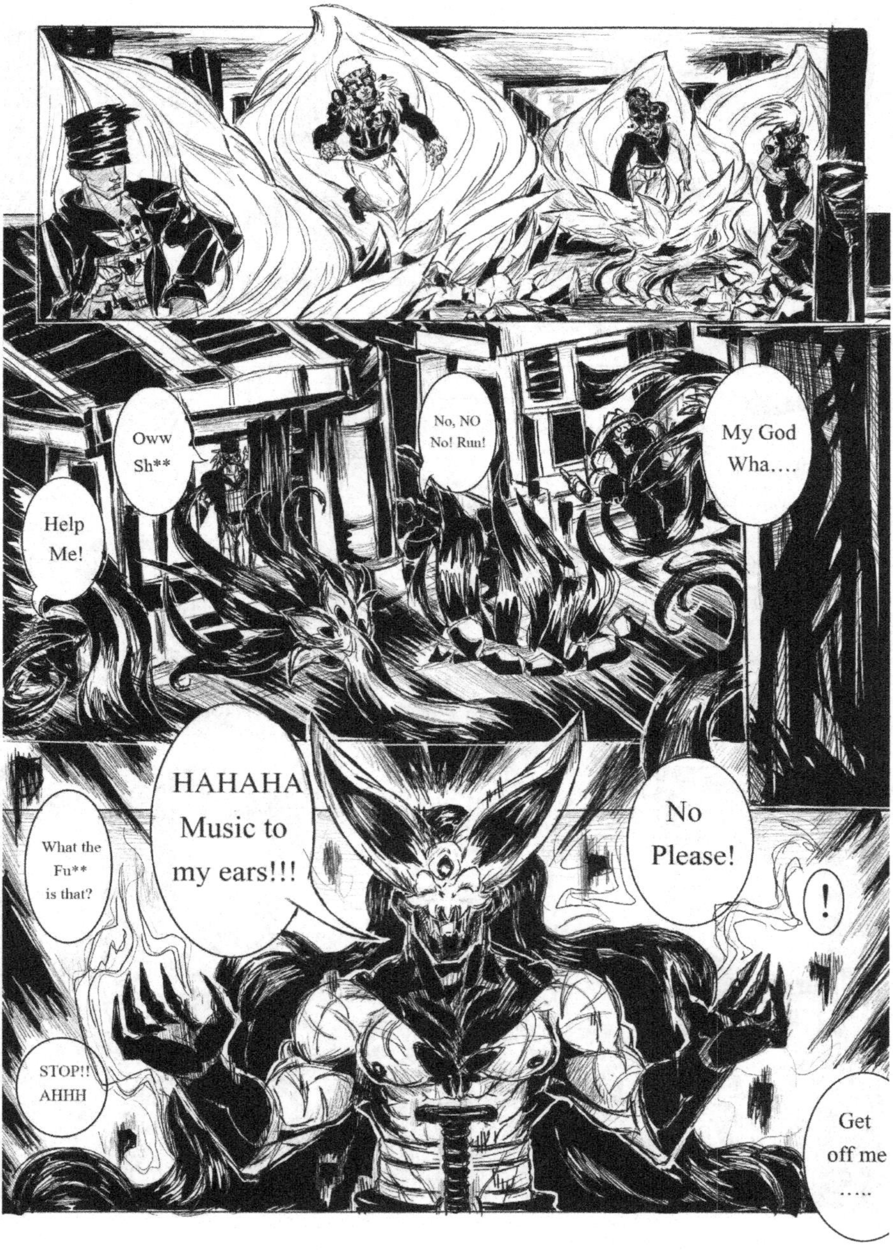
Oww
Sh**
Help
Me!
No, NO
No! Run!
My God
Wha....
What the
Fu**
is that?
HAHAHA
Music to
my ears!!!
No
Please!
!
STOP!!
AHHH
Get
off me
.....

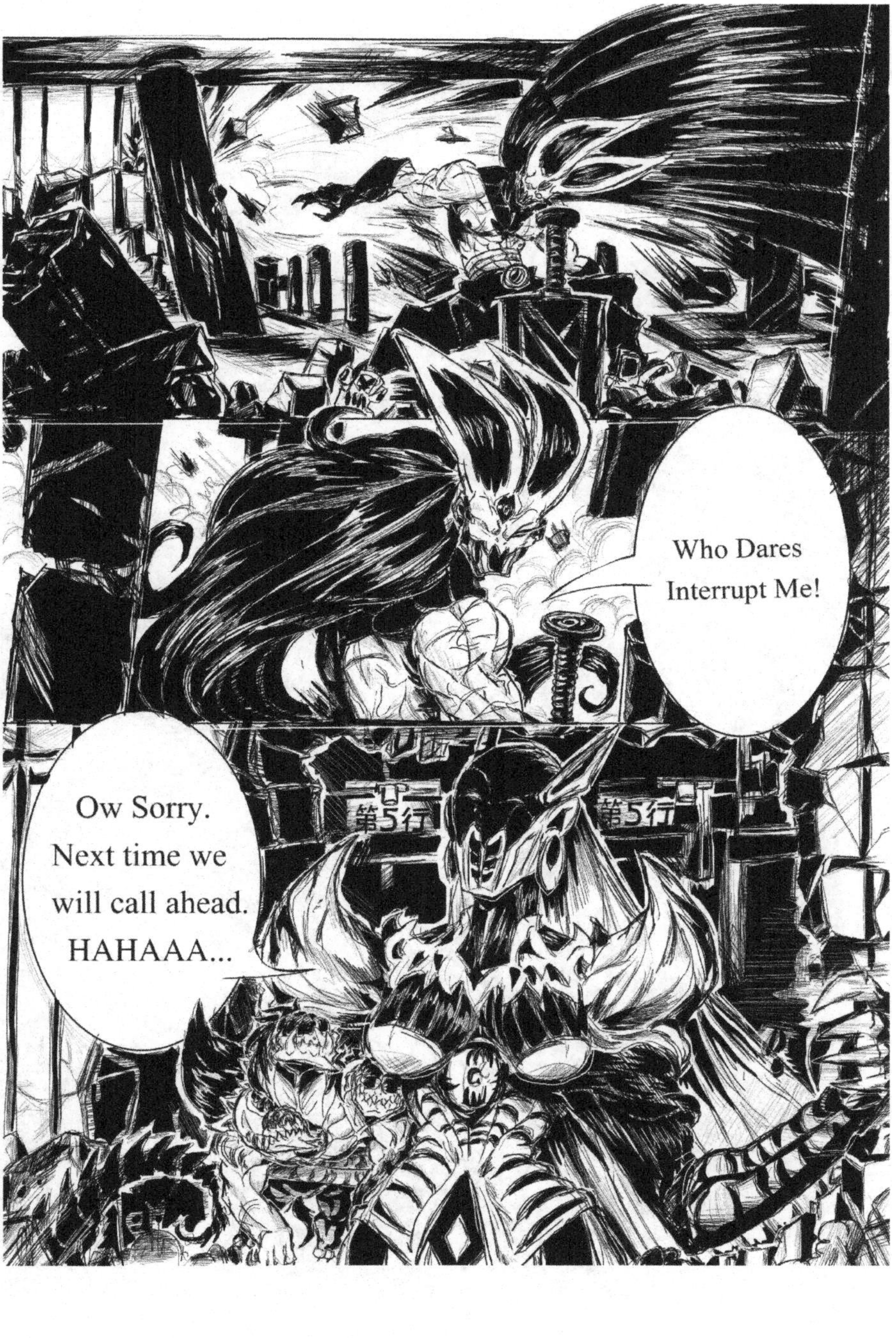
Who Dares Interrupt Me!
Ow Sorry. Next time we will call ahead. HAHAAA...
第5行
第5行

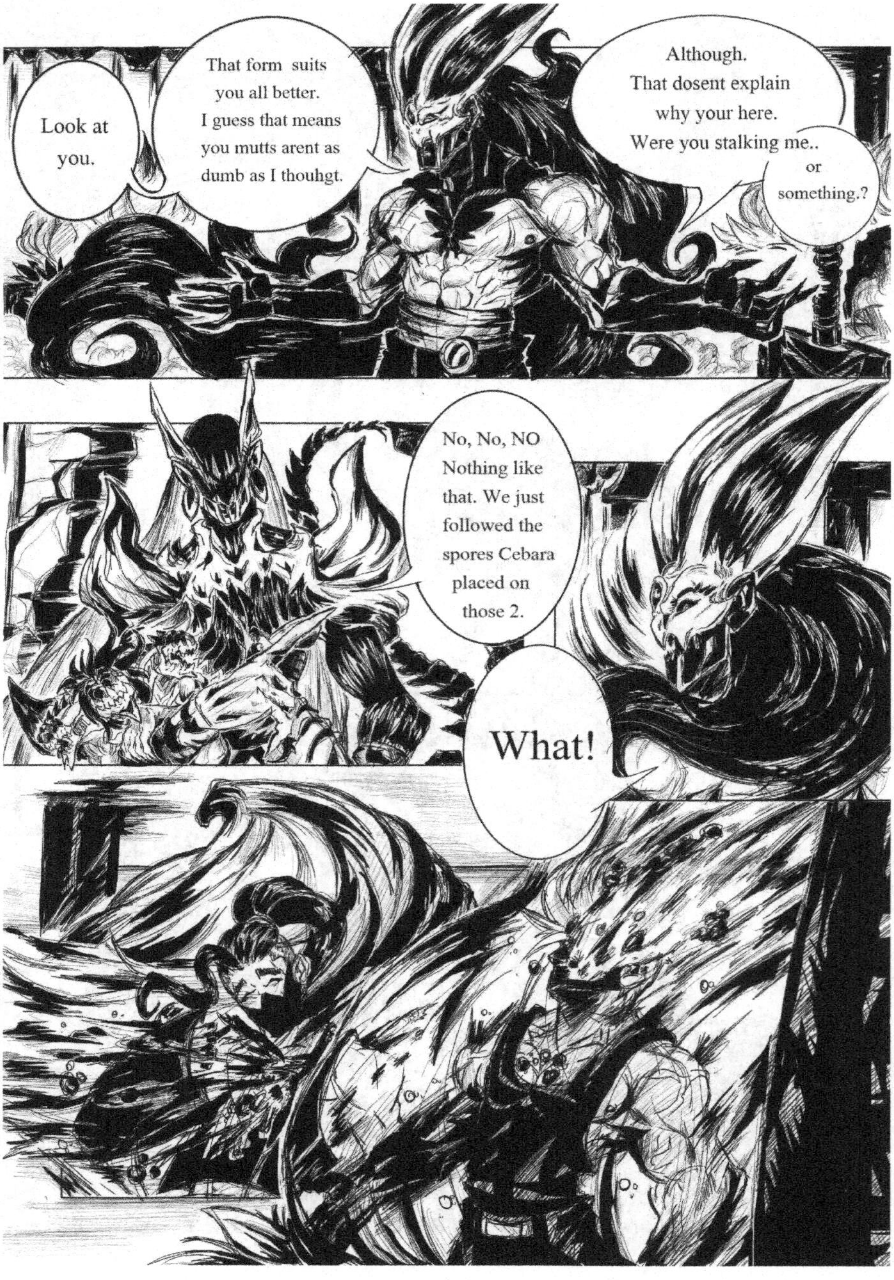

Look at you.
That form suits you all better. I guess that means you mutts arent as dumb as I thouhgt.
Although. That dosent explain why your here. Were you stalking me..
or something.?
No, No, NO Nothing like that. We just followed the spores Cebara placed on those 2.
What!

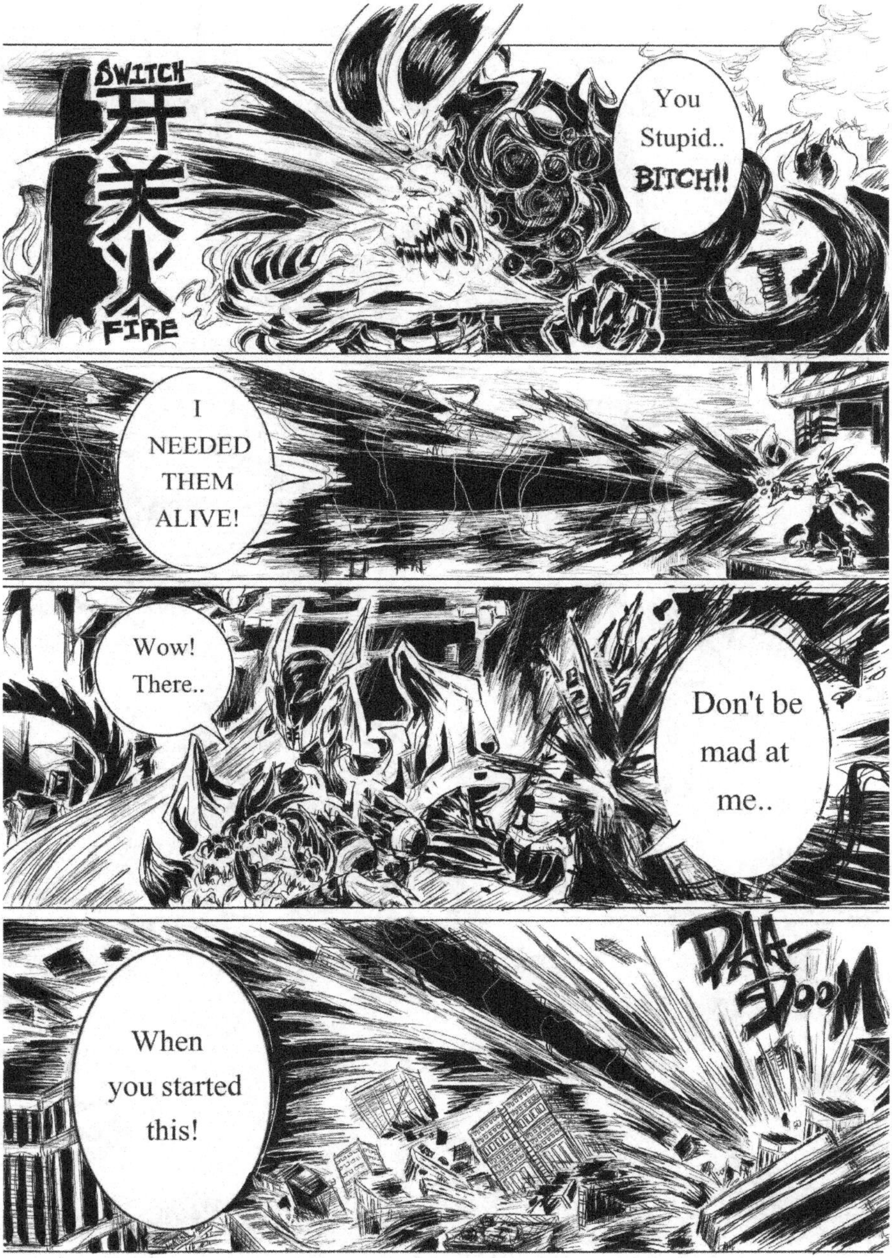
SWITCH
开关火
FIRE
You Stupid.. BITCH!!
I NEEDED THEM ALIVE!
Wow! There..
Don't be mad at me..
DAA-DOOM
When you started this!

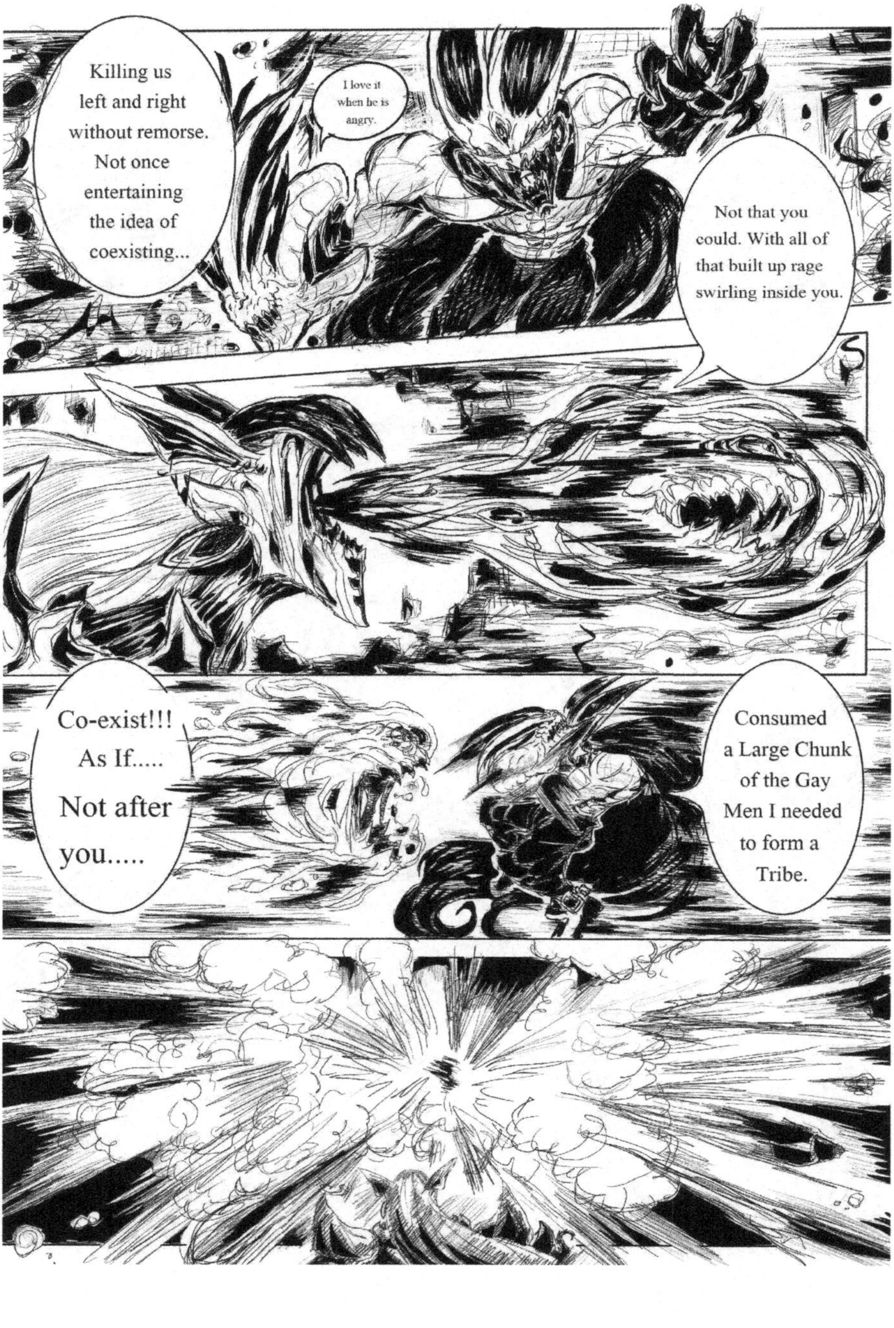
Killing us left and right without remorse. Not once entertaining the idea of coexisting...
I love it when he is angry.
Not that you could. With all of that built up rage swirling inside you.
Co-exist!!! As If..... Not after you.....
Consumed a Large Chunk of the Gay Men I needed to form a Tribe.

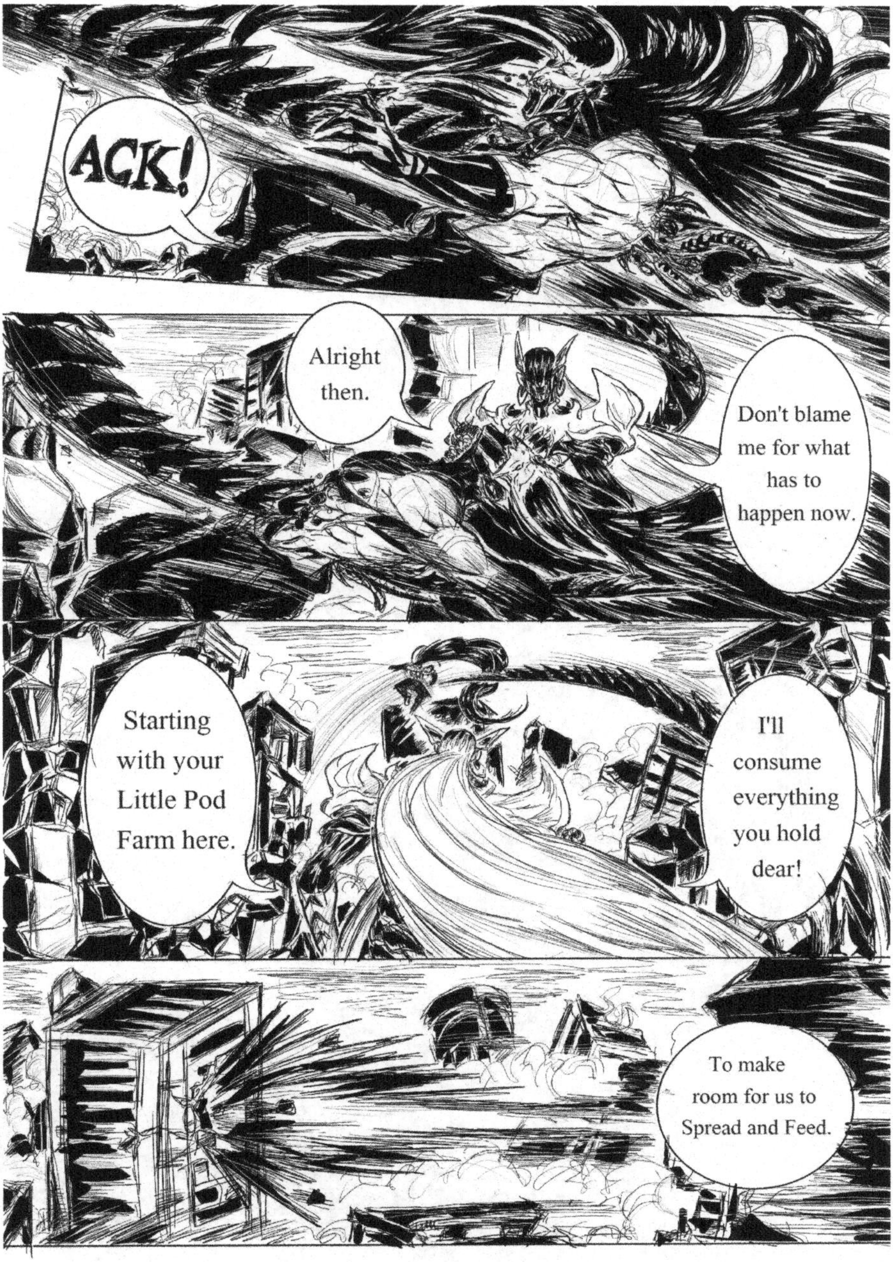
ACK!
Alright then.
Don't blame me for what has to happen now.
Starting with your Little Pod Farm here.
I'll consume everything you hold dear!
To make room for us to Spread and Feed.

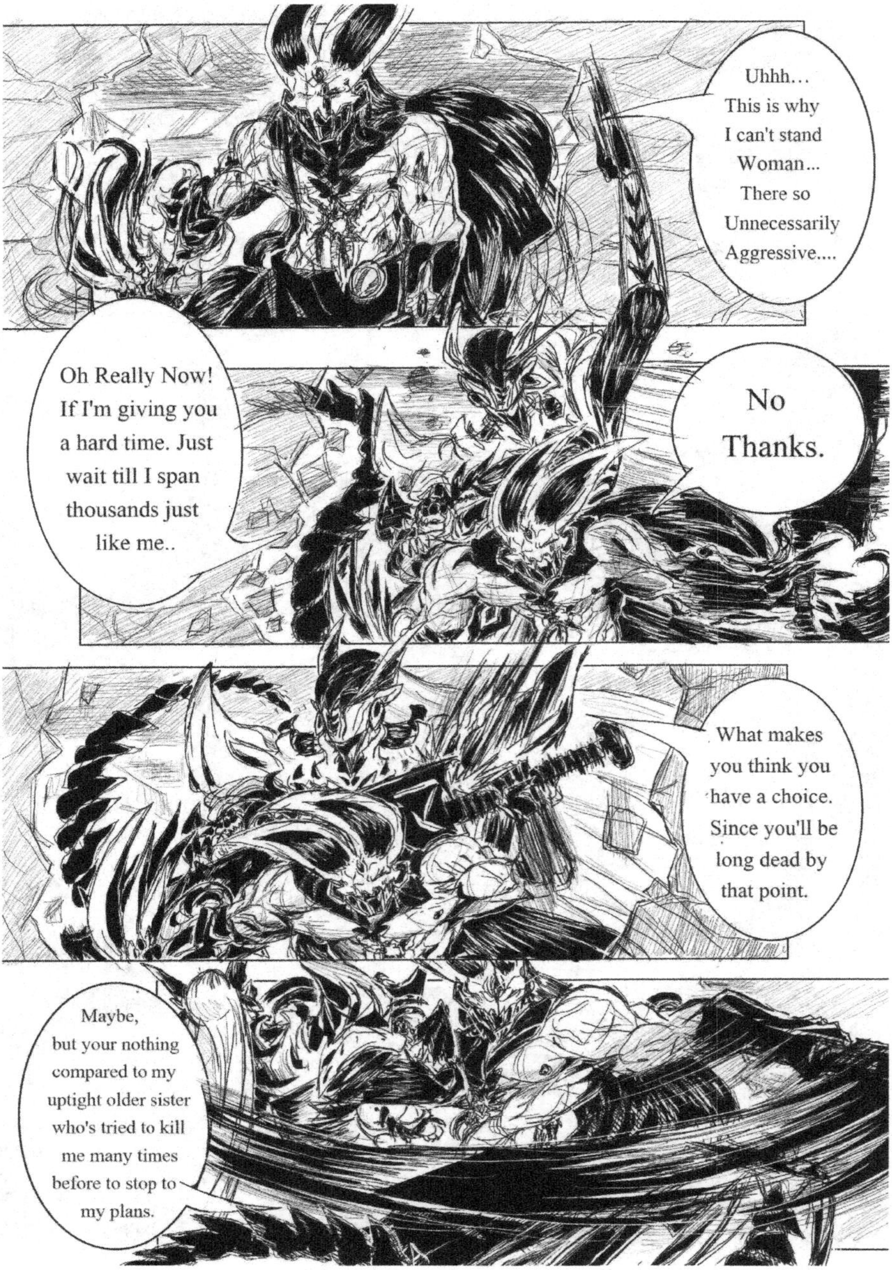
Uhhh…
This is why
I can't stand
Woman...
There so
Unnecessarily
Aggressive....
Oh Really Now!
If I'm giving you
a hard time. Just
wait till I span
thousands just
like me..
No
Thanks.
What makes
you think you
have a choice.
Since you'll be
long dead by
that point.
Maybe,
but your nothing
compared to my
uptight older sister
who's tried to kill
me many times
before to stop to
my plans.

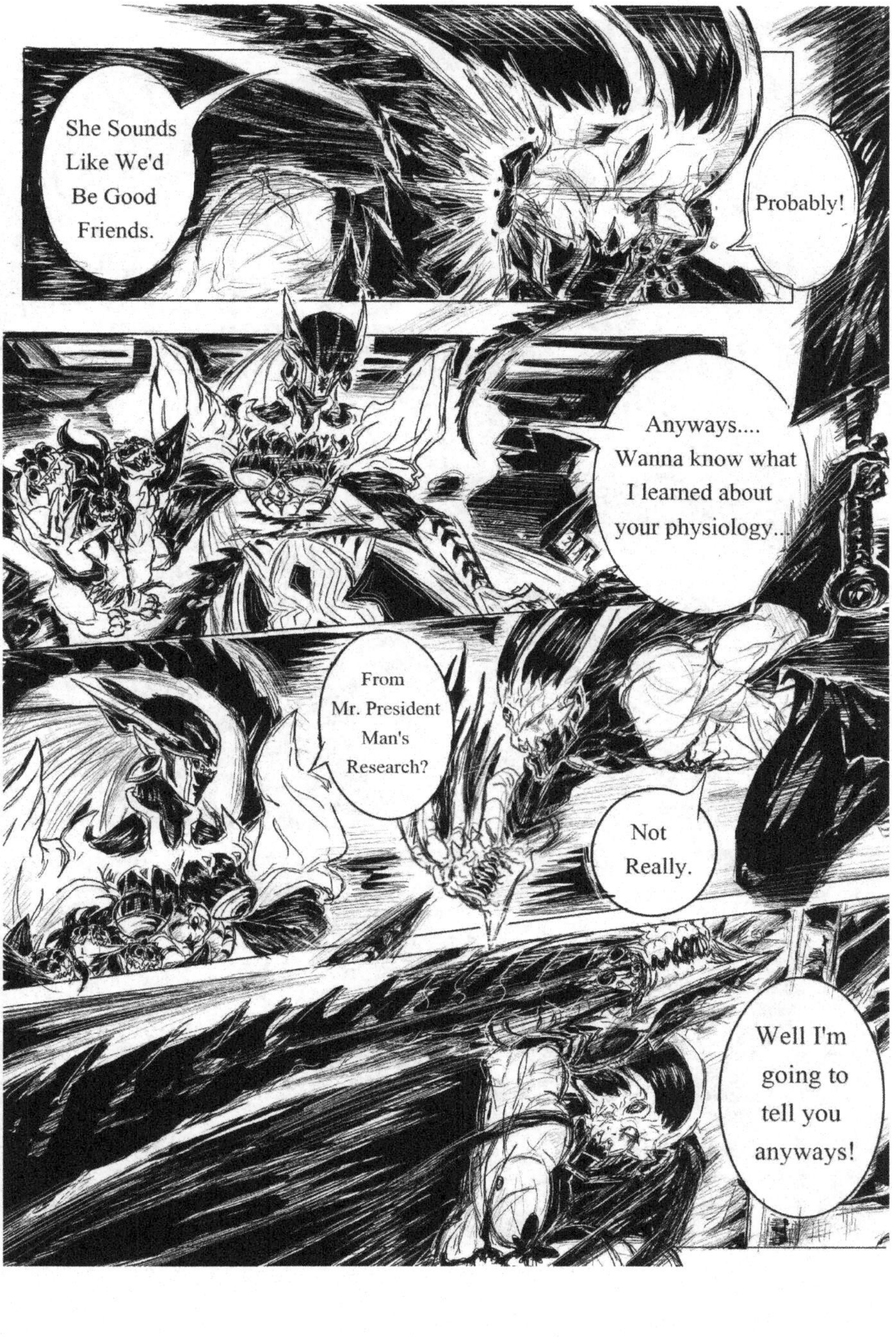
She Sounds Like We'd Be Good Friends.
Probably!
Anyways.... Wanna know what I learned about your physiology..
From Mr. President Man's Research?
Not Really.
Well I'm going to tell you anyways!

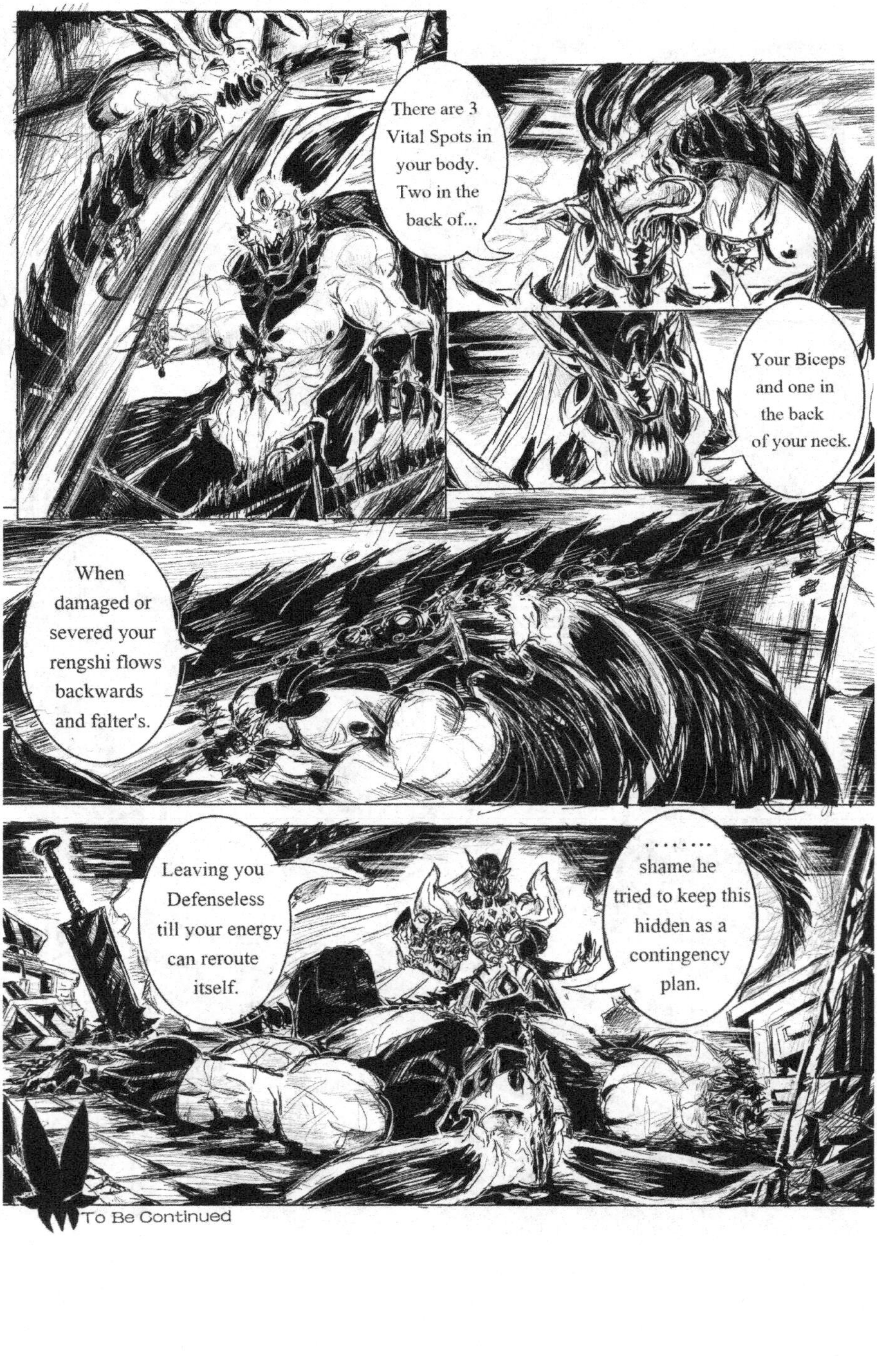
There are 3 Vital Spots in your body. Two in the back of...
Your Biceps and one in the back of your neck.
When damaged or severed your rengshi flows backwards and falter's.
Leaving you Defenseless till your energy can reroute itself.
.... shame he tried to keep this hidden as a contingency plan.
To Be Continued

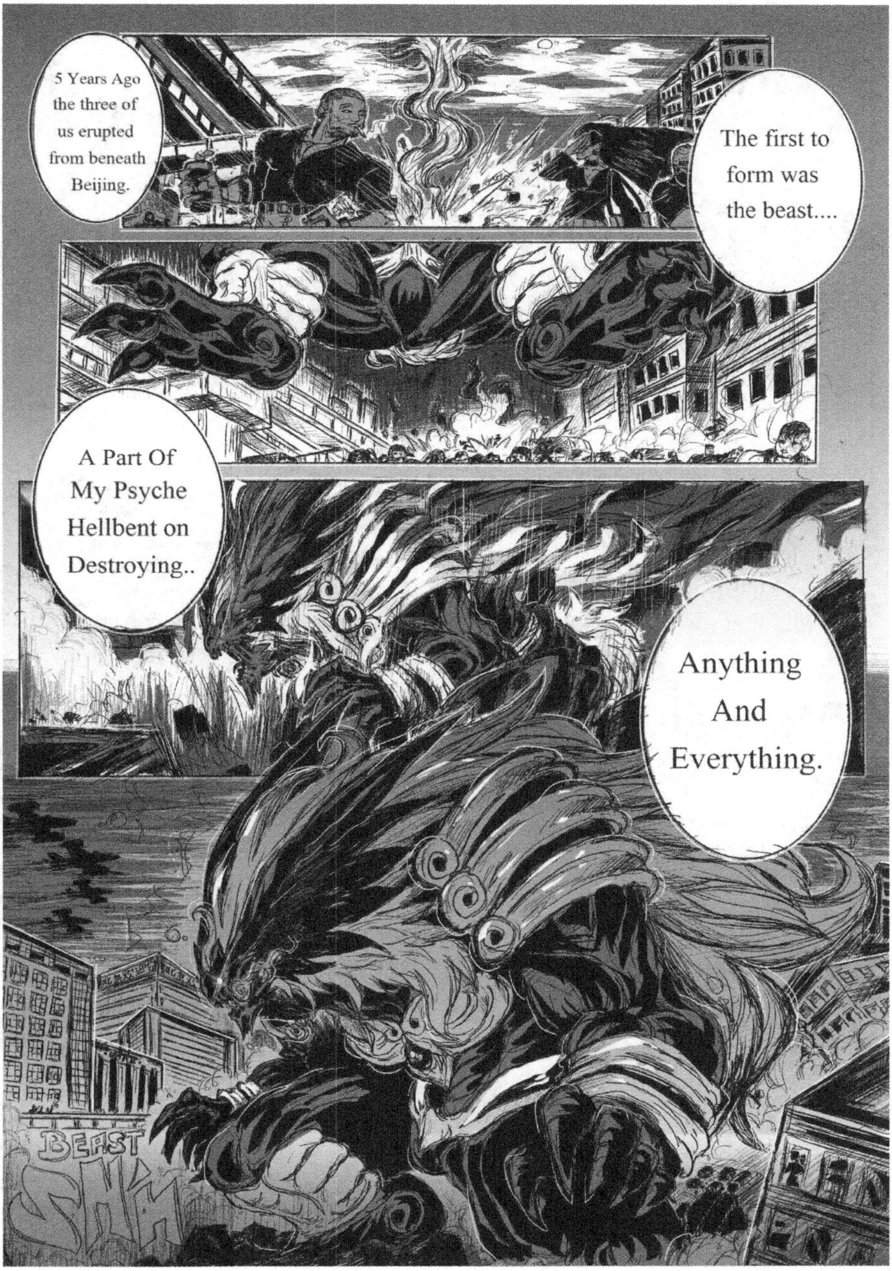
5 Years Ago the three of us erupted from beneath Beijing.
The first to form was the beast....
A Part Of My Psyche Hellbent on Destroying..
Anything And Everything.
BEAST

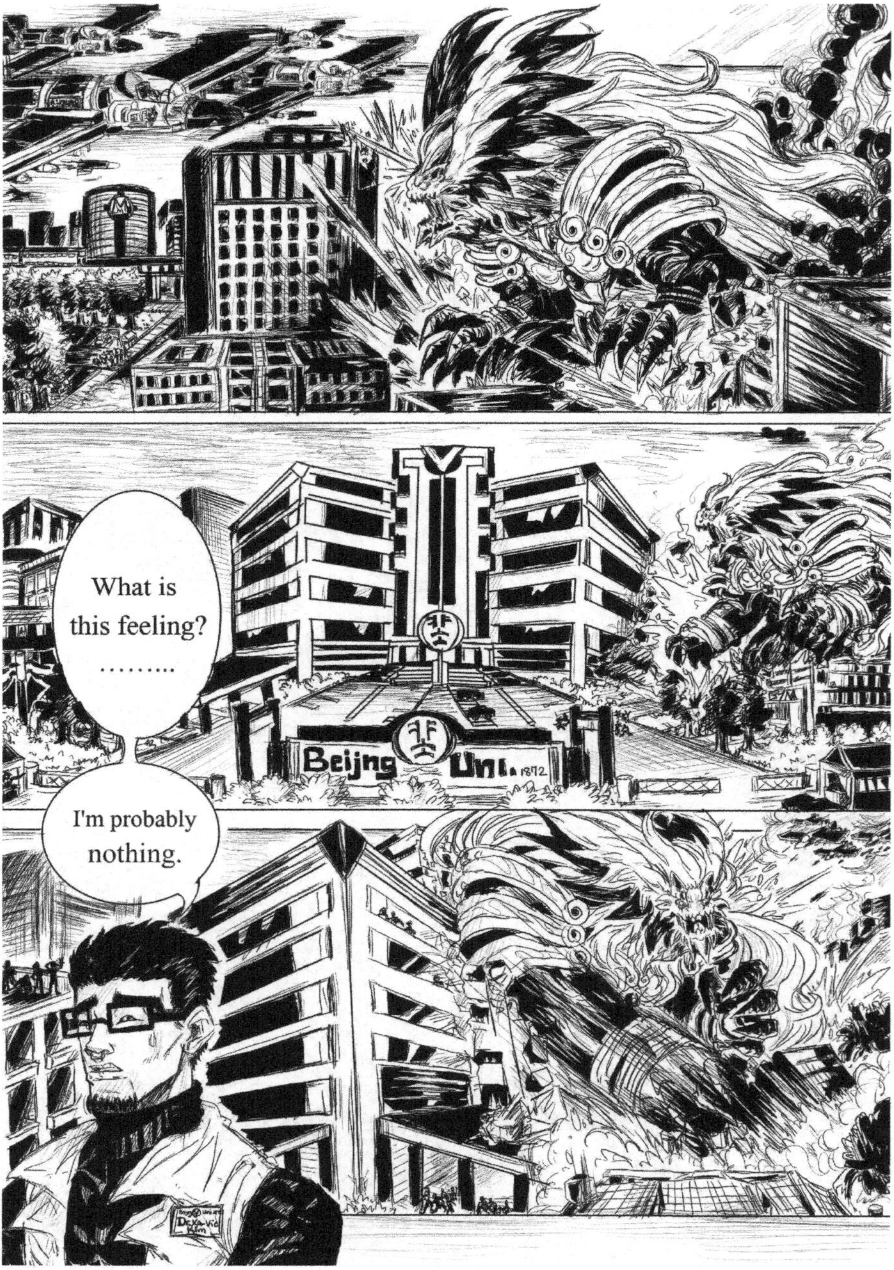

What is this feeling?
……....
I'm probably nothing.
Beijng Uni. 1872

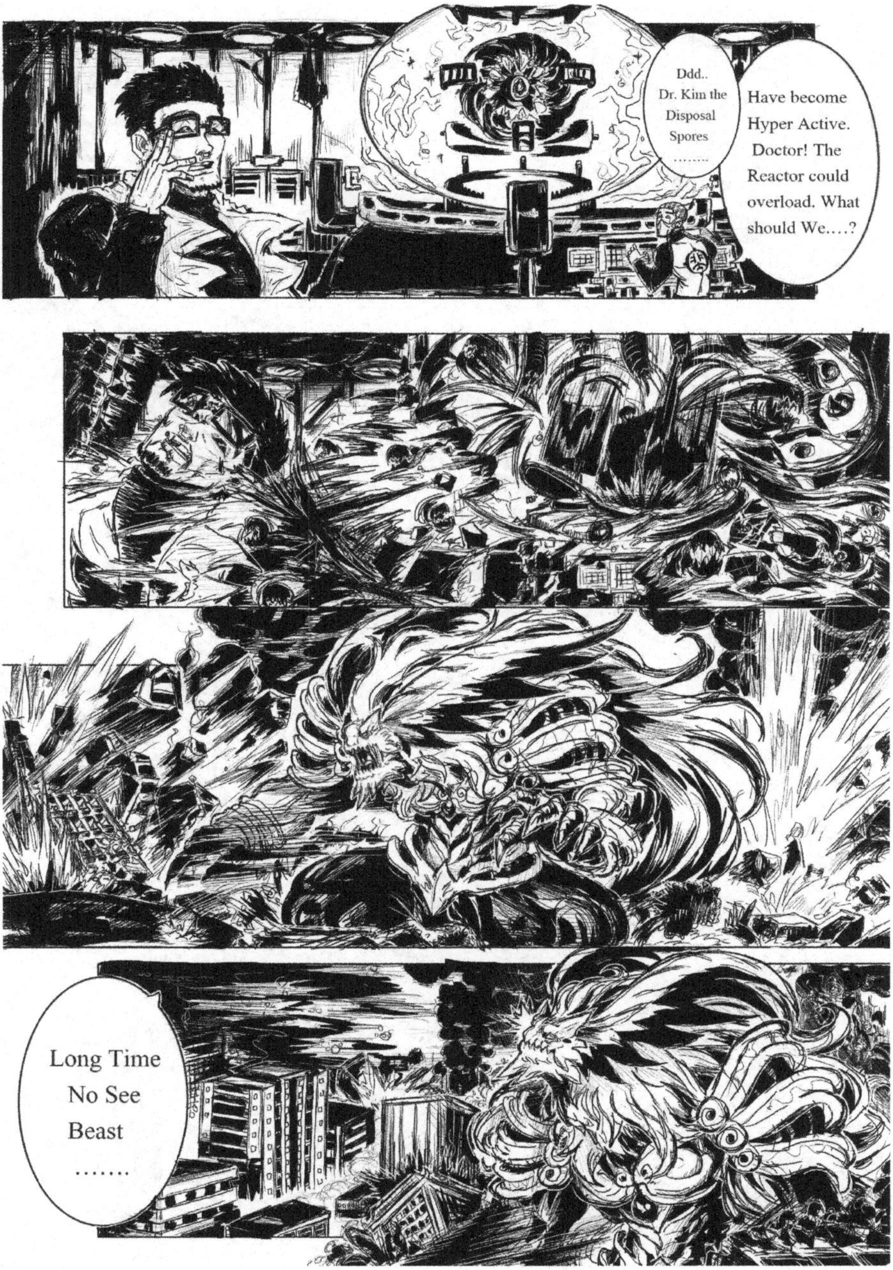
Ddd.. Dr. Kim the Disposal Spores ....
Have become Hyper Active. Doctor! The Reactor could overload. What should We....?
Long Time No See Beast ....

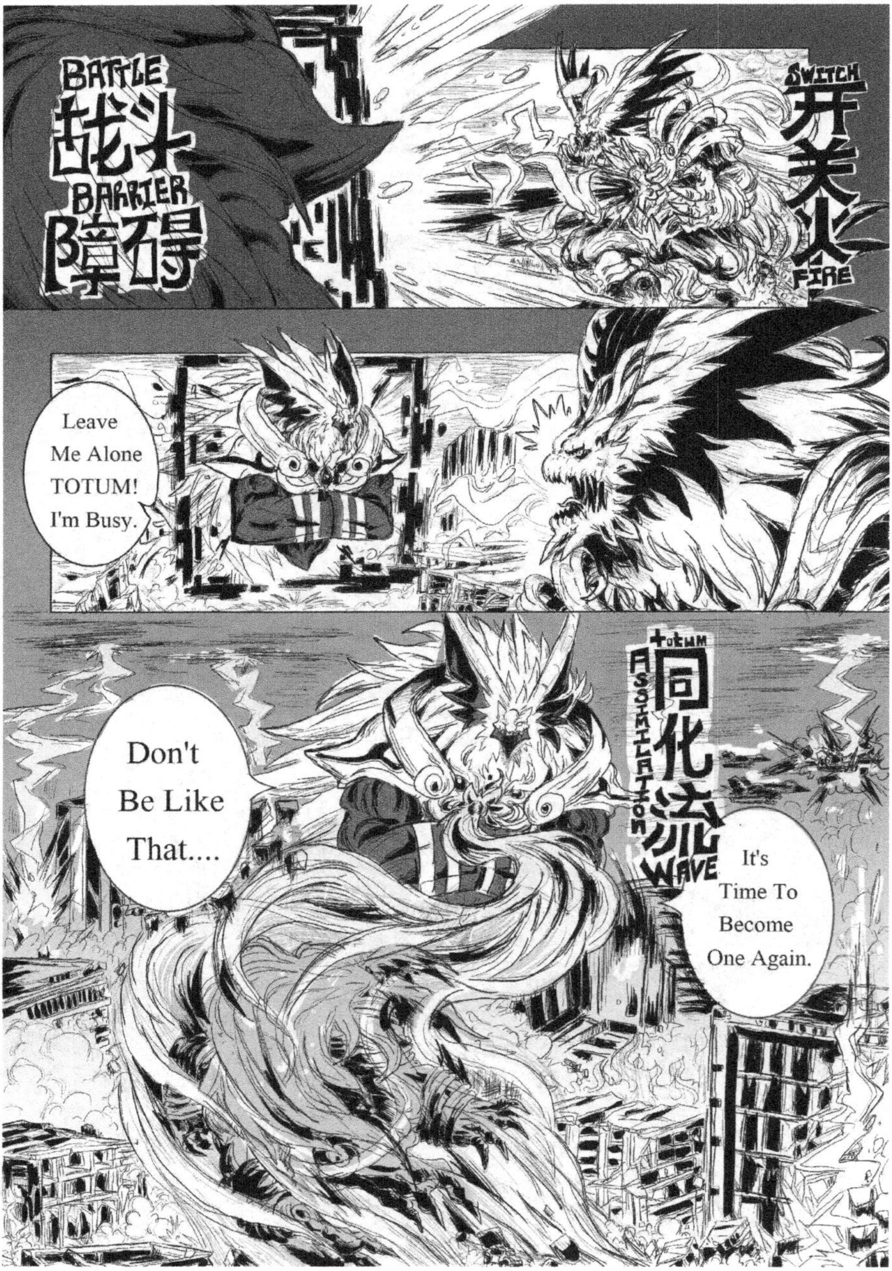
BATTLE
战斗
BARRIER
障碍
SWITCH
开关火
FIRE
Leave Me Alone TOTUM! I'm Busy.
Don't Be Like That....
TOTUM
ASSIMILATION
同化流
WAVE
It's Time To Become One Again.

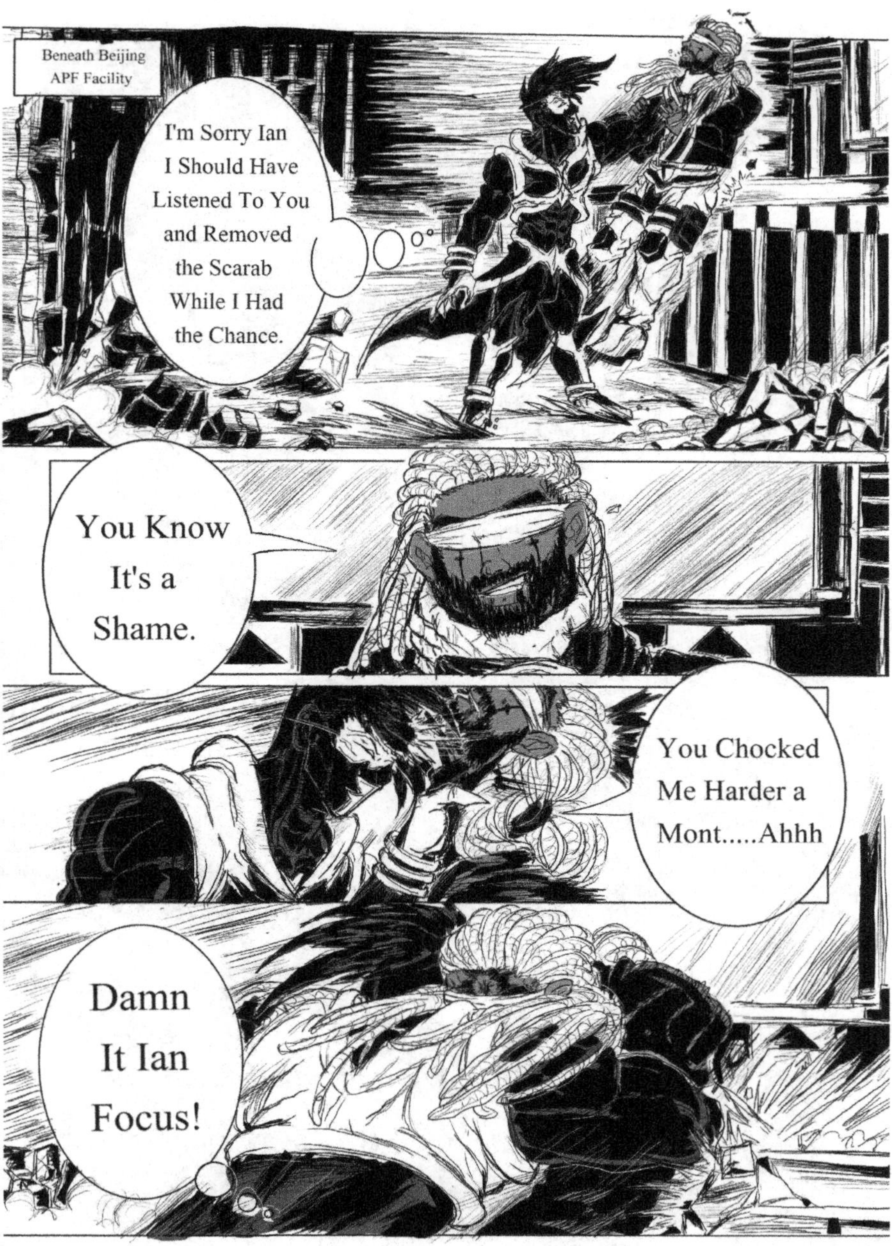
Beneath Beijing
APF Facility
I'm Sorry Ian I Should Have Listened To You and Removed the Scarab While I Had the Chance.
You Know It's a Shame.
You Chocked Me Harder a Mont.....Ahhh
Damn It Ian Focus!

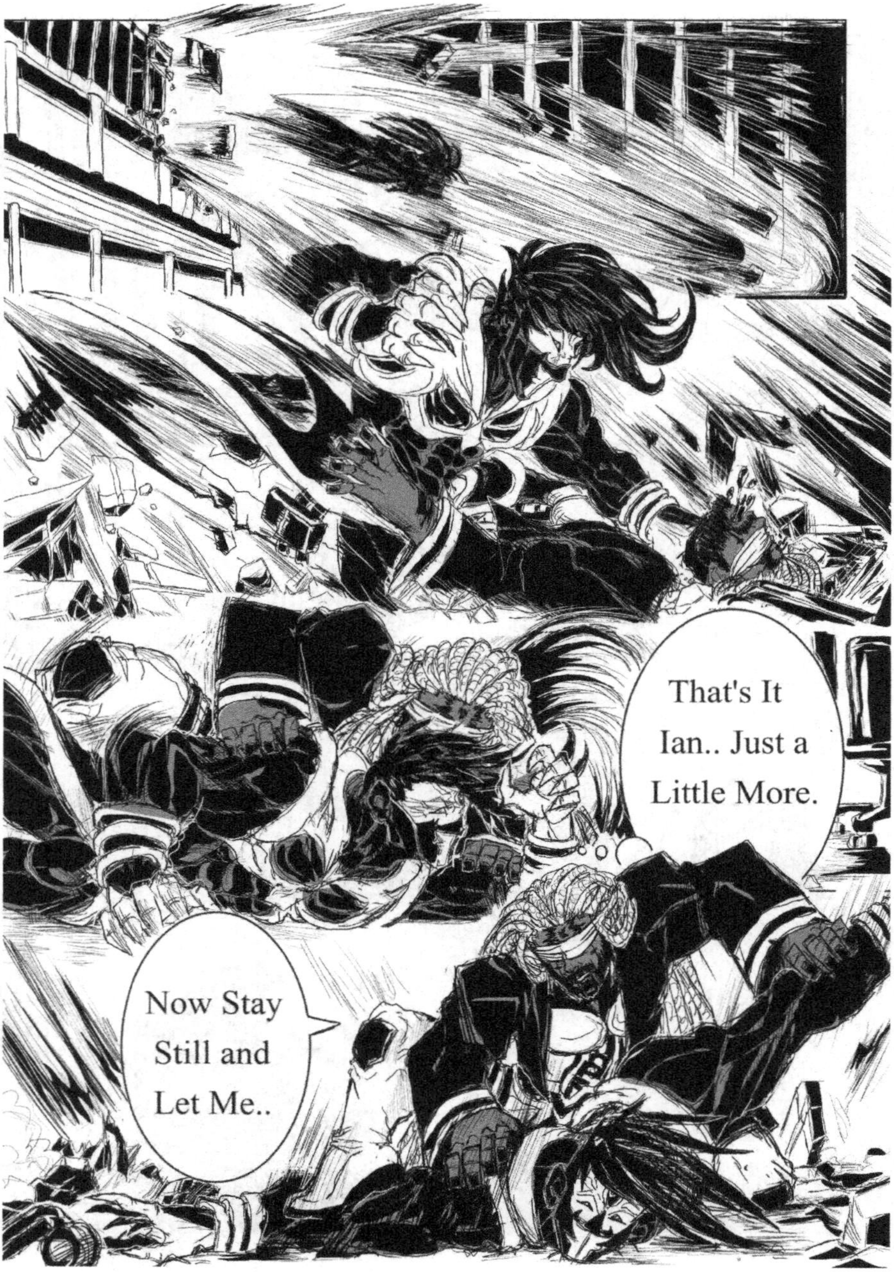
That's It Ian.. Just a Little More.
Now Stay Still and Let Me..

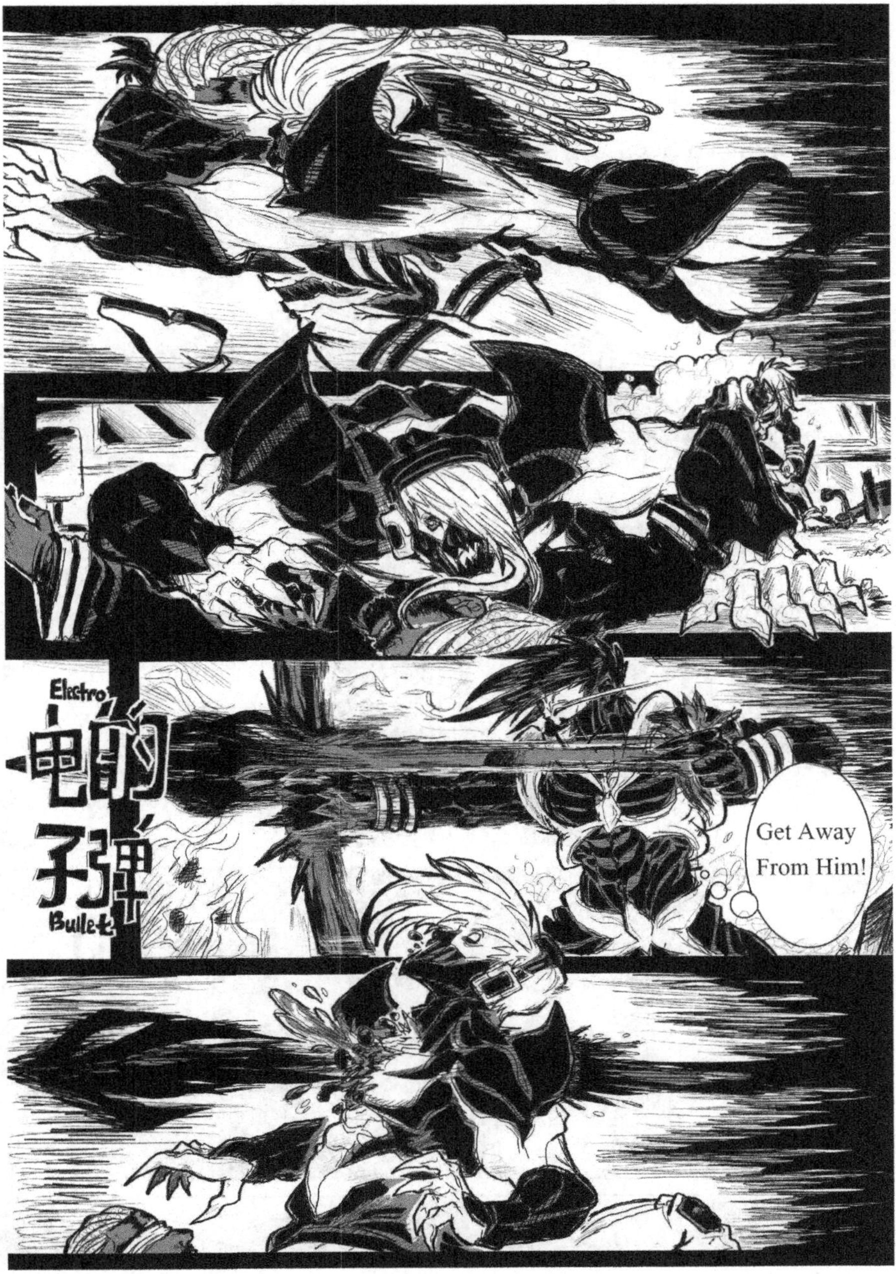
Electro
电的子弹
Bullet
Get Away From Him!

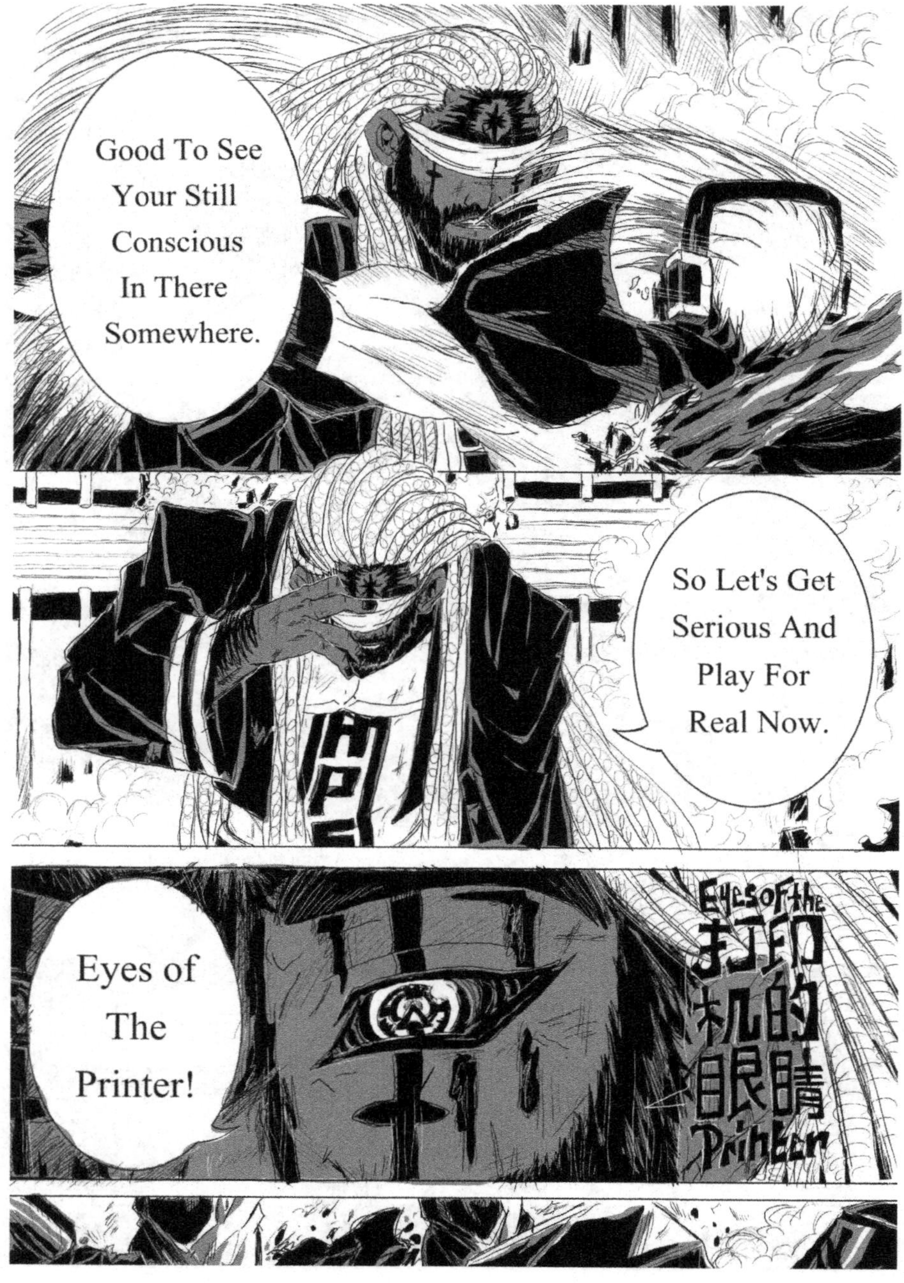
Good To See Your Still Conscious In There Somewhere.
So Let's Get Serious And Play For Real Now.
Eyes of The Printer!
Eyes of the 打印机的眼睛 Printer

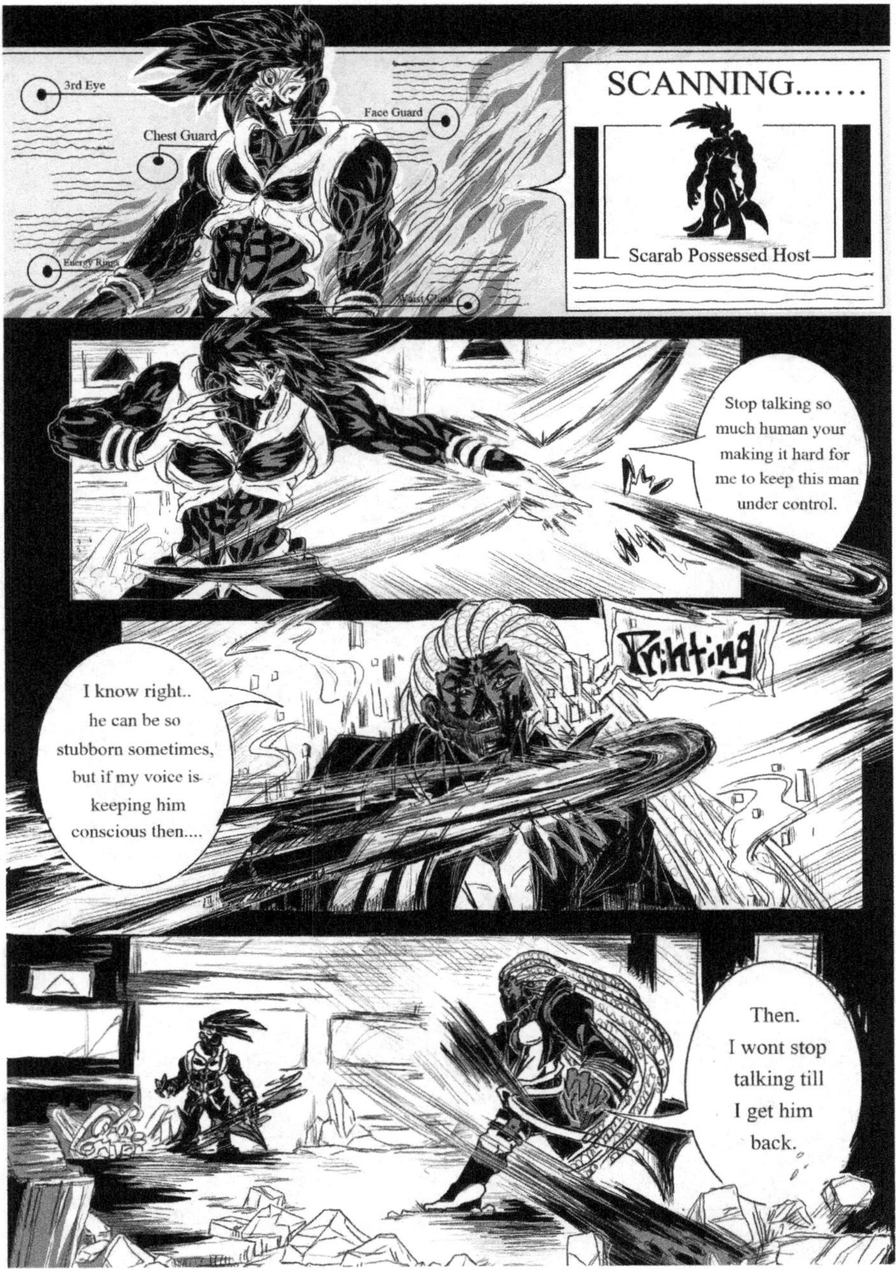
3rd Eye
Face Guard
Chest Guard
Energy Rings
Waist Cloak
SCANNING.......
Scarab Possessed Host
Stop talking so much human your making it hard for me to keep this man under control.
Printing
I know right.. he can be so stubborn sometimes, but if my voice is keeping him conscious then....
Then. I wont stop talking till I get him back.

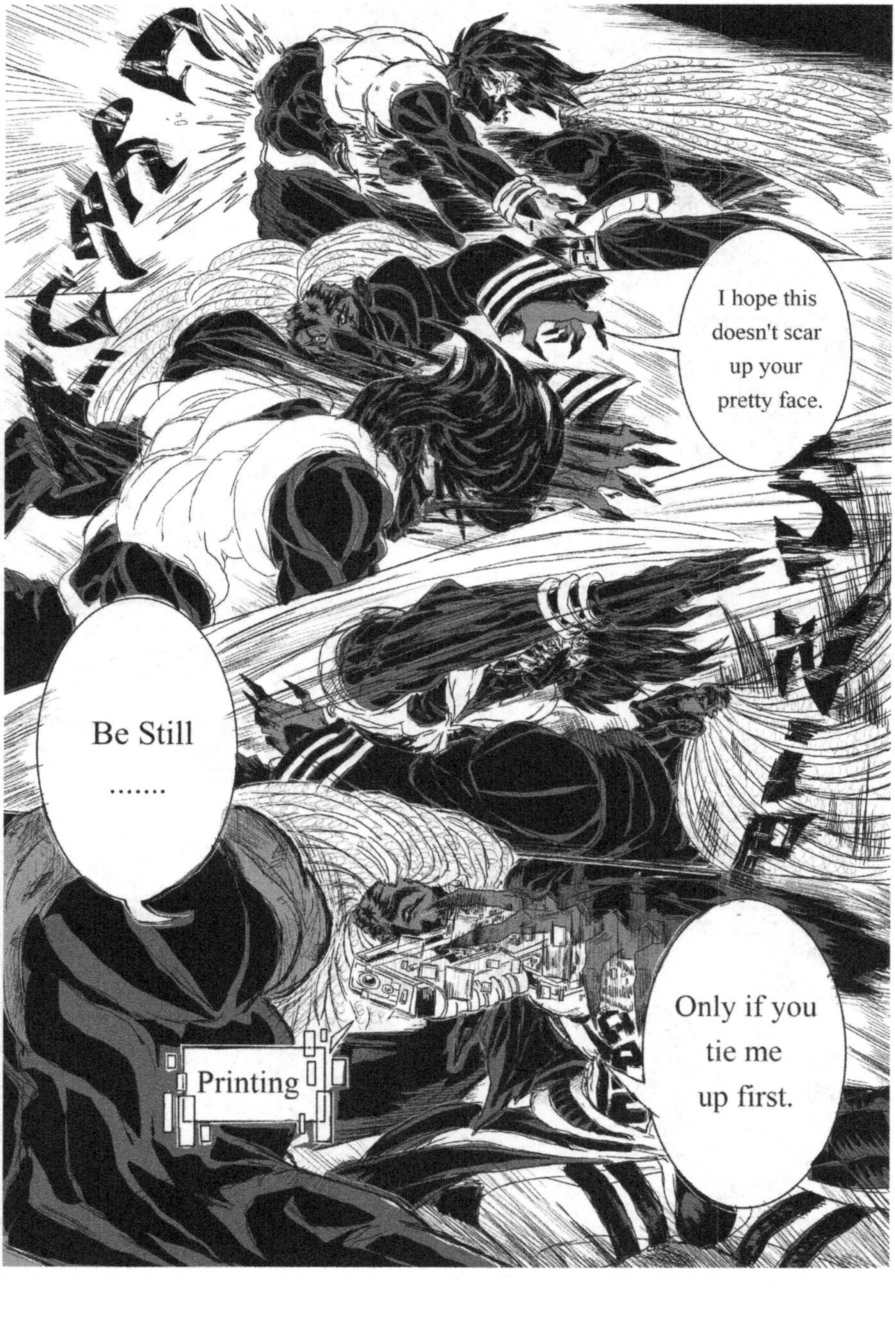
I hope this doesn't scar up your pretty face.
Be Still ....
Only if you tie me up first.
Printing

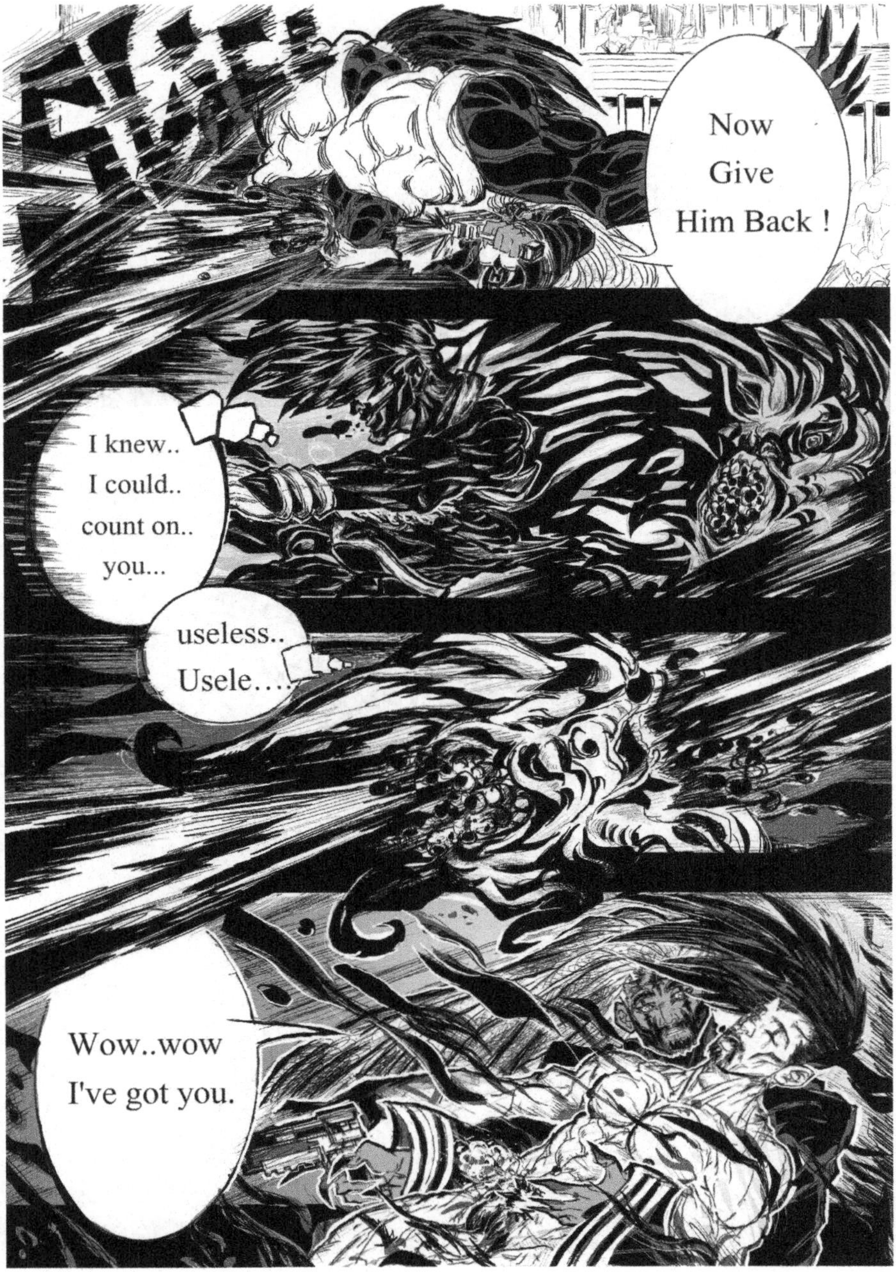
Now Give Him Back !
I knew.. I could.. count on.. you...
useless.. Usele….
Wow..wow I've got you.

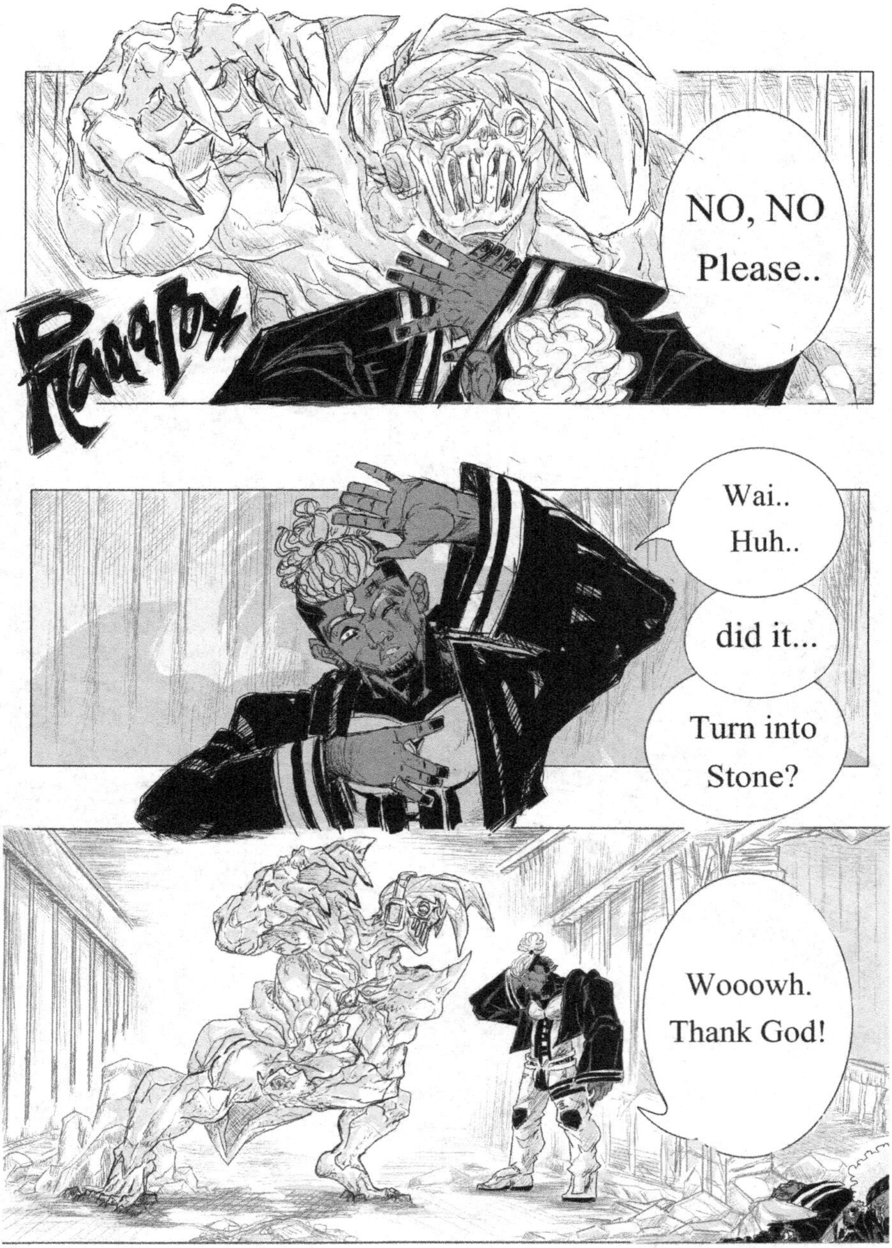
NO, NO
Please..
Wai..
Huh..
did it...
Turn into
Stone?
Wooowh.
Thank God!

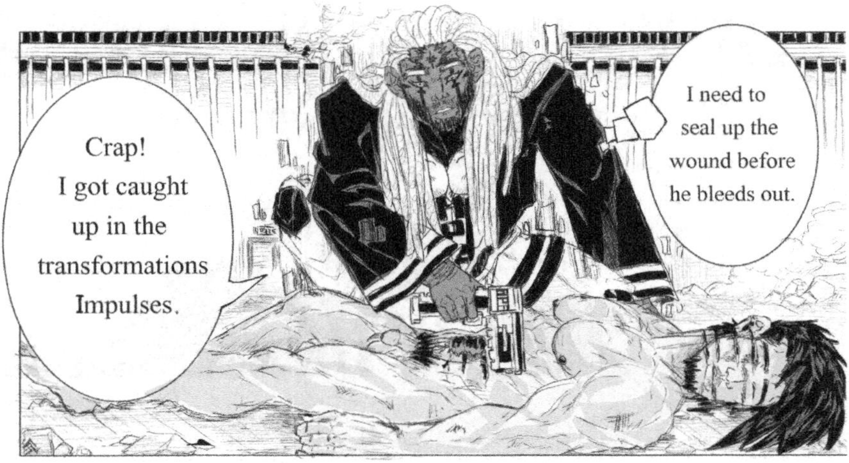
Crap! I got caught up in the transformations Impulses.
I need to seal up the wound before he bleeds out.

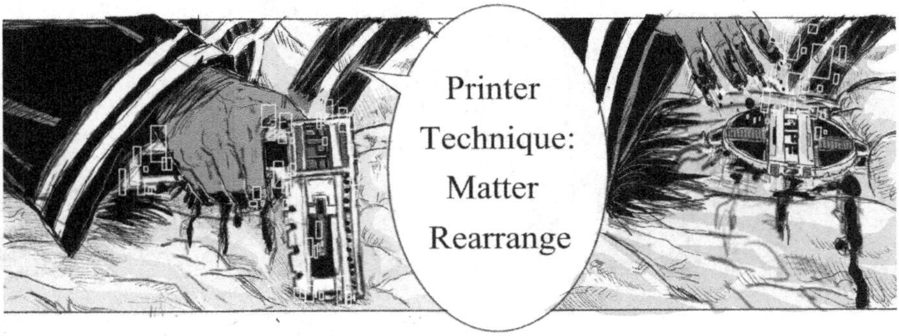
Printer Technique: Matter Rearrange

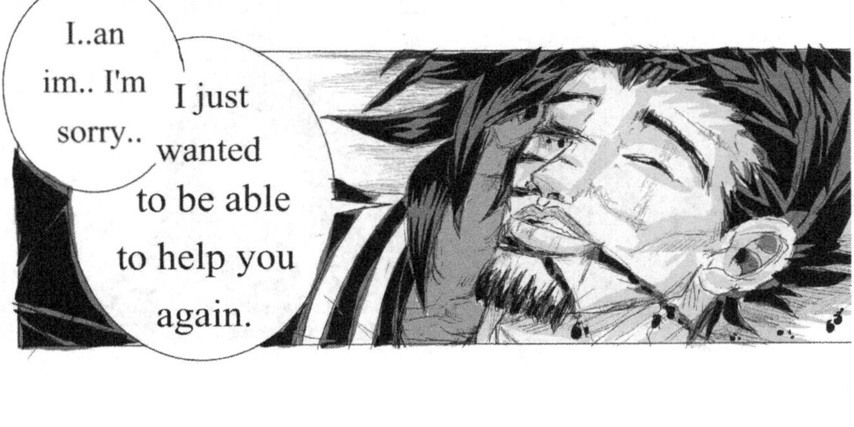
I..an im.. I'm sorry..
I just wanted to be able to help you again.

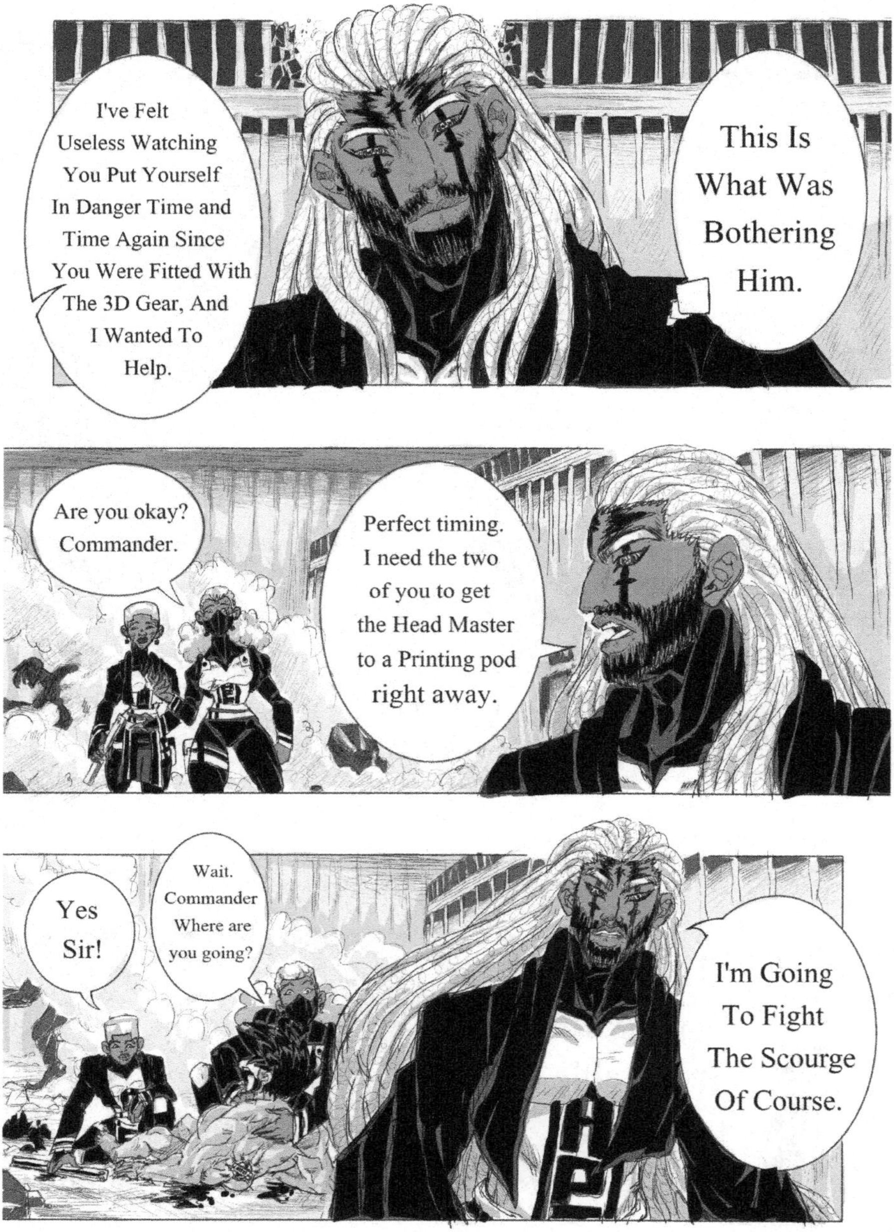
I've Felt Useless Watching You Put Yourself In Danger Time and Time Again Since You Were Fitted With The 3D Gear, And I Wanted To Help.
This Is What Was Bothering Him.
Are you okay? Commander.
Perfect timing. I need the two of you to get the Head Master to a Printing pod right away.
Yes Sir!
Wait. Commander Where are you going?
I'm Going To Fight The Scourge Of Course.

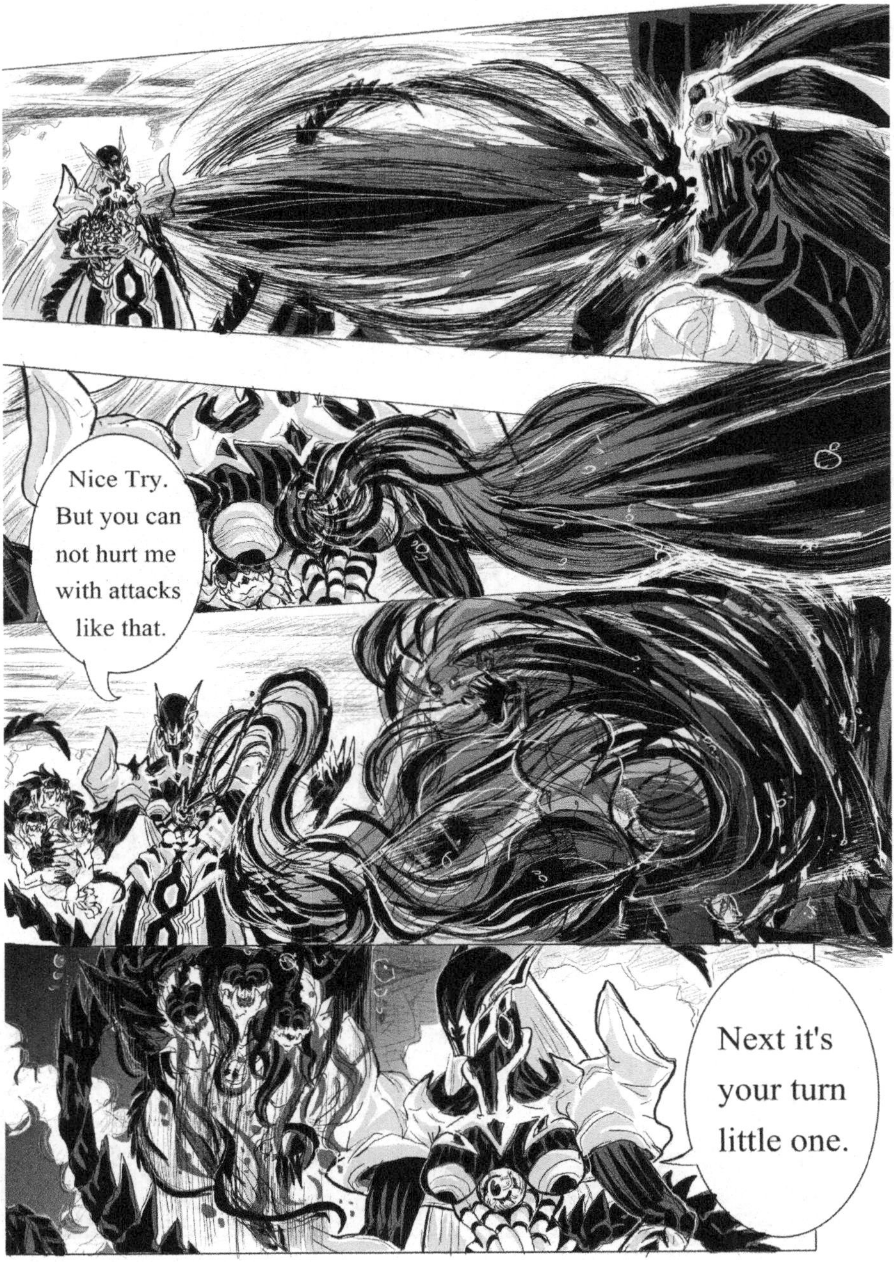
Nice Try. But you can not hurt me with attacks like that.
Next it's your turn little one.

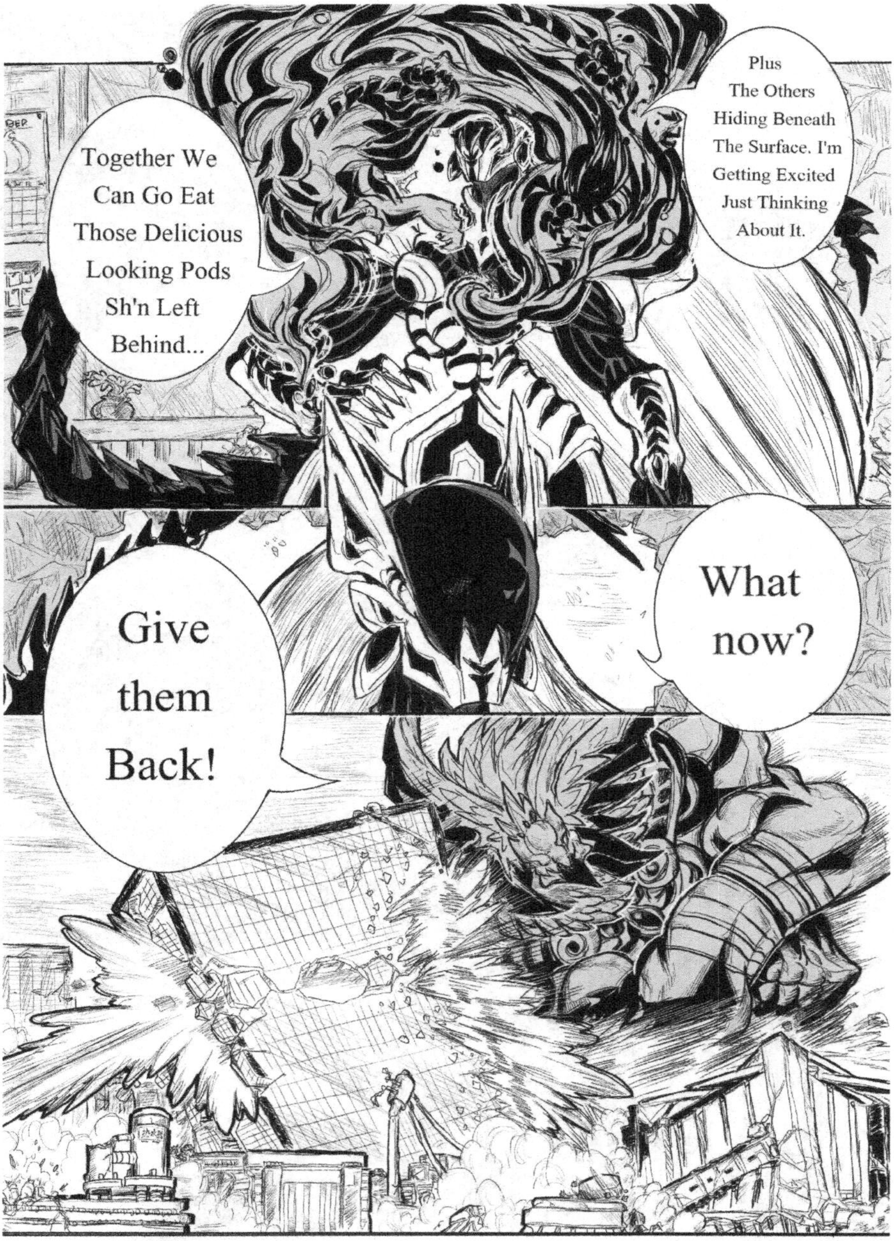
Together We Can Go Eat Those Delicious Looking Pods Sh'n Left Behind...
Plus The Others Hiding Beneath The Surface. I'm Getting Excited Just Thinking About It.
Give them Back!
What now?

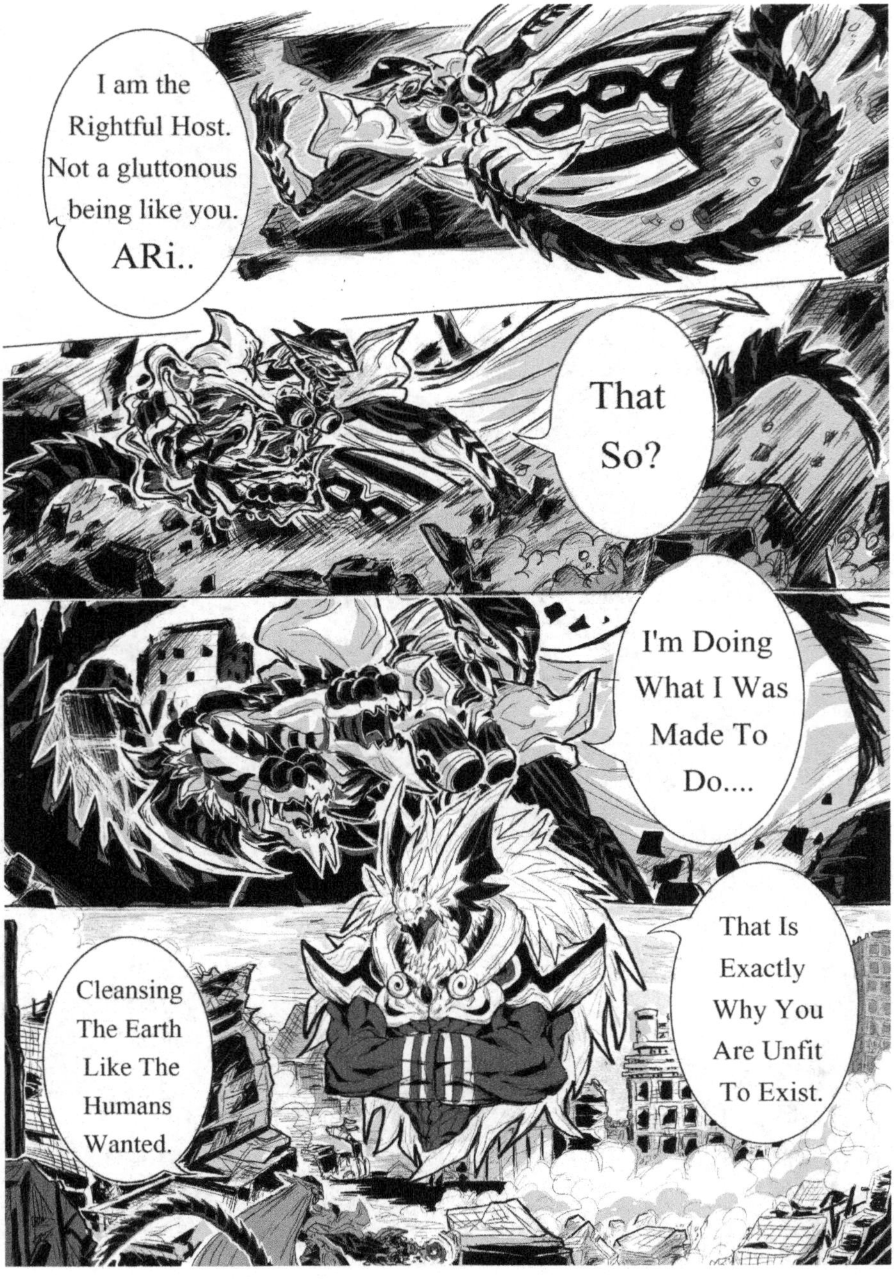
I am the Rightful Host. Not a gluttonous being like you. ARi..
That So?
I'm Doing What I Was Made To Do....
Cleansing The Earth Like The Humans Wanted.
That Is Exactly Why You Are Unfit To Exist.

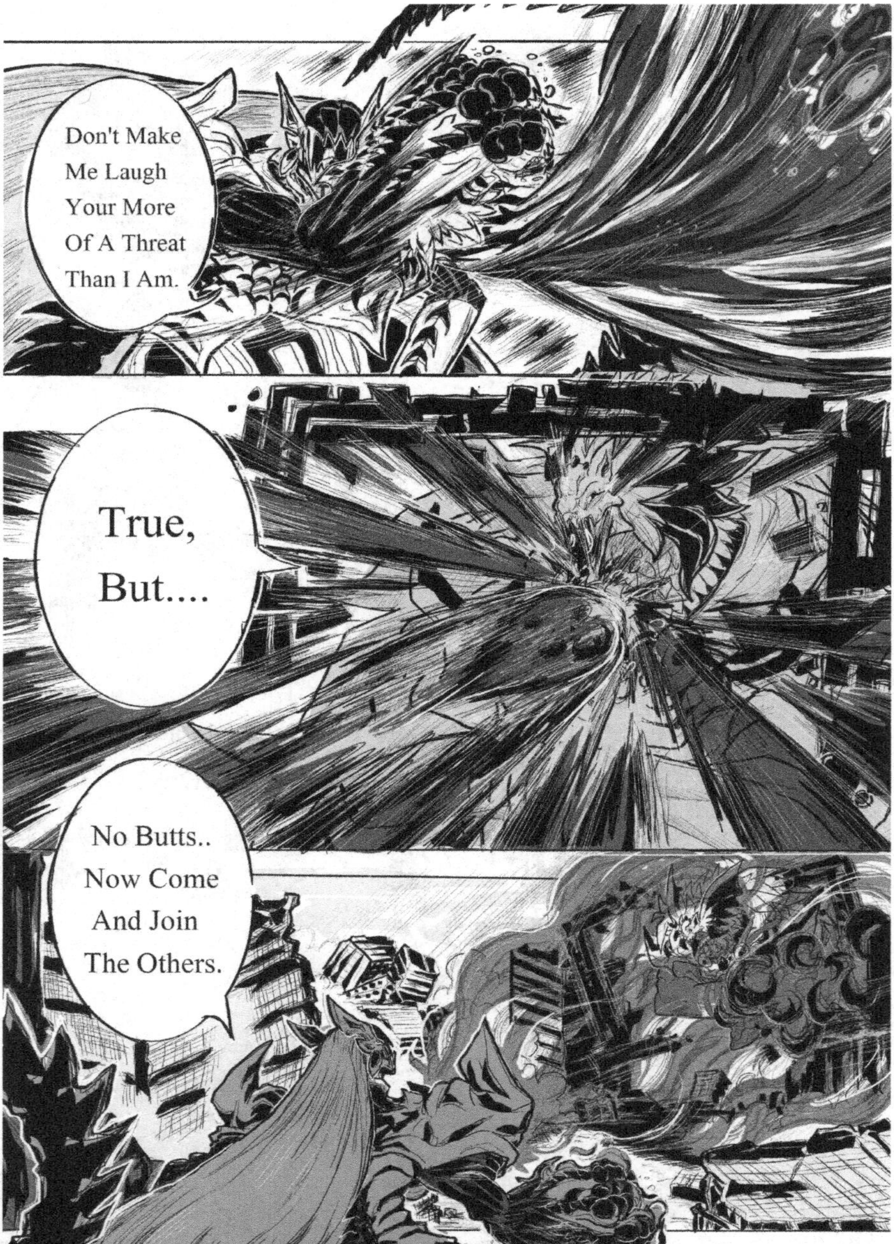
Don't Make Me Laugh Your More Of A Threat Than I Am.
True, But....
No Butts.. Now Come And Join The Others.

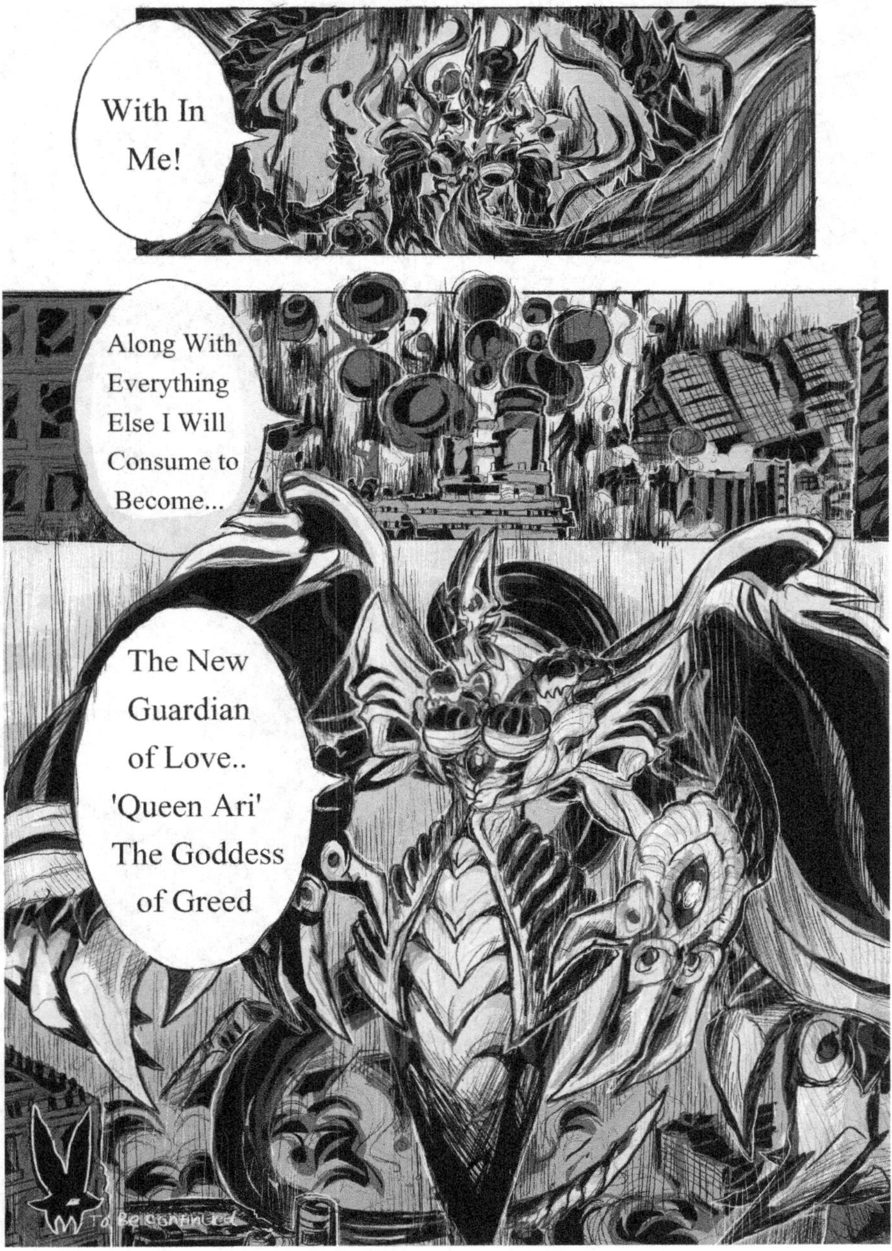
With In Me!
Along With Everything Else I Will Consume to Become...
The New Guardian of Love.. 'Queen Ari' The Goddess of Greed
To Be Continued

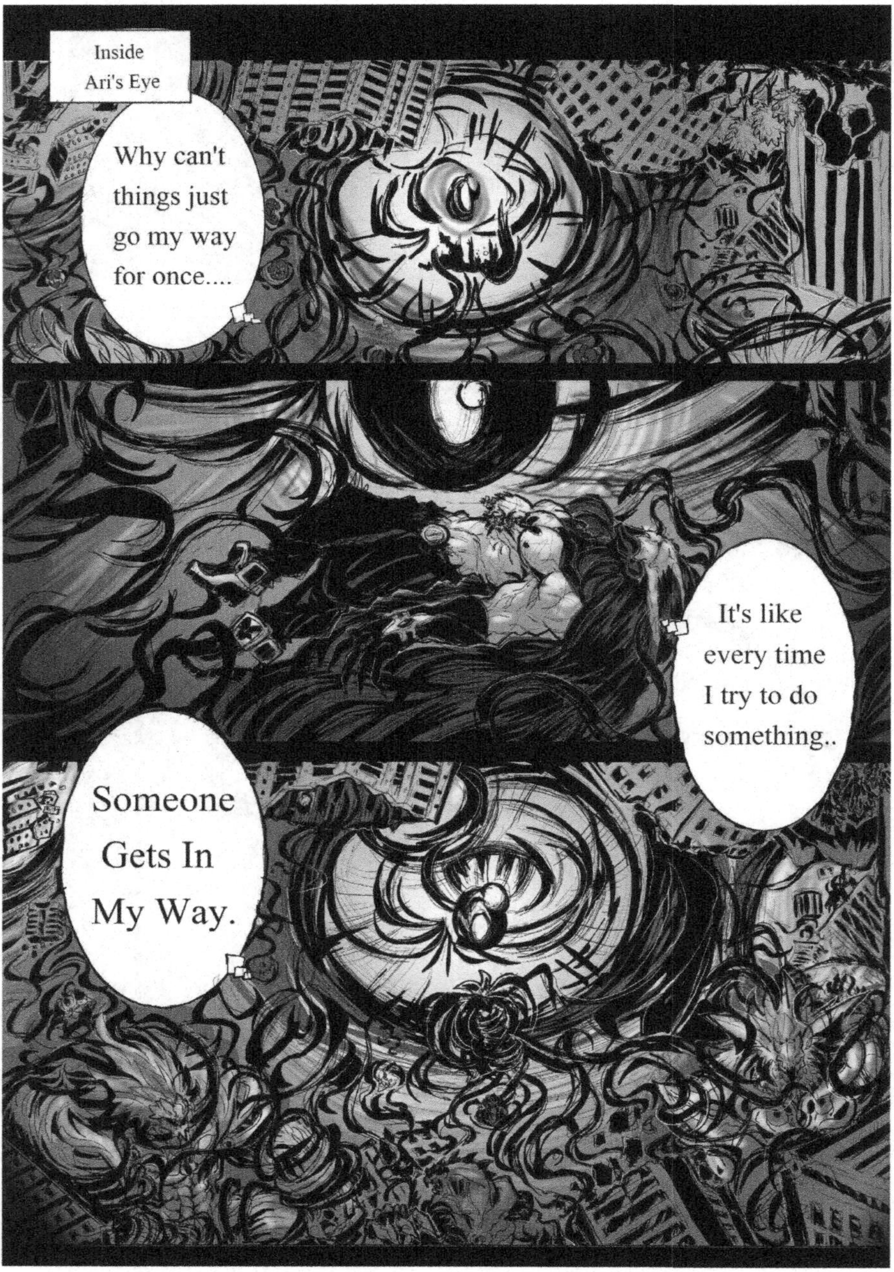
Inside Ari's Eye
Why can't things just go my way for once....
It's like every time I try to do something..
Someone Gets In My Way.

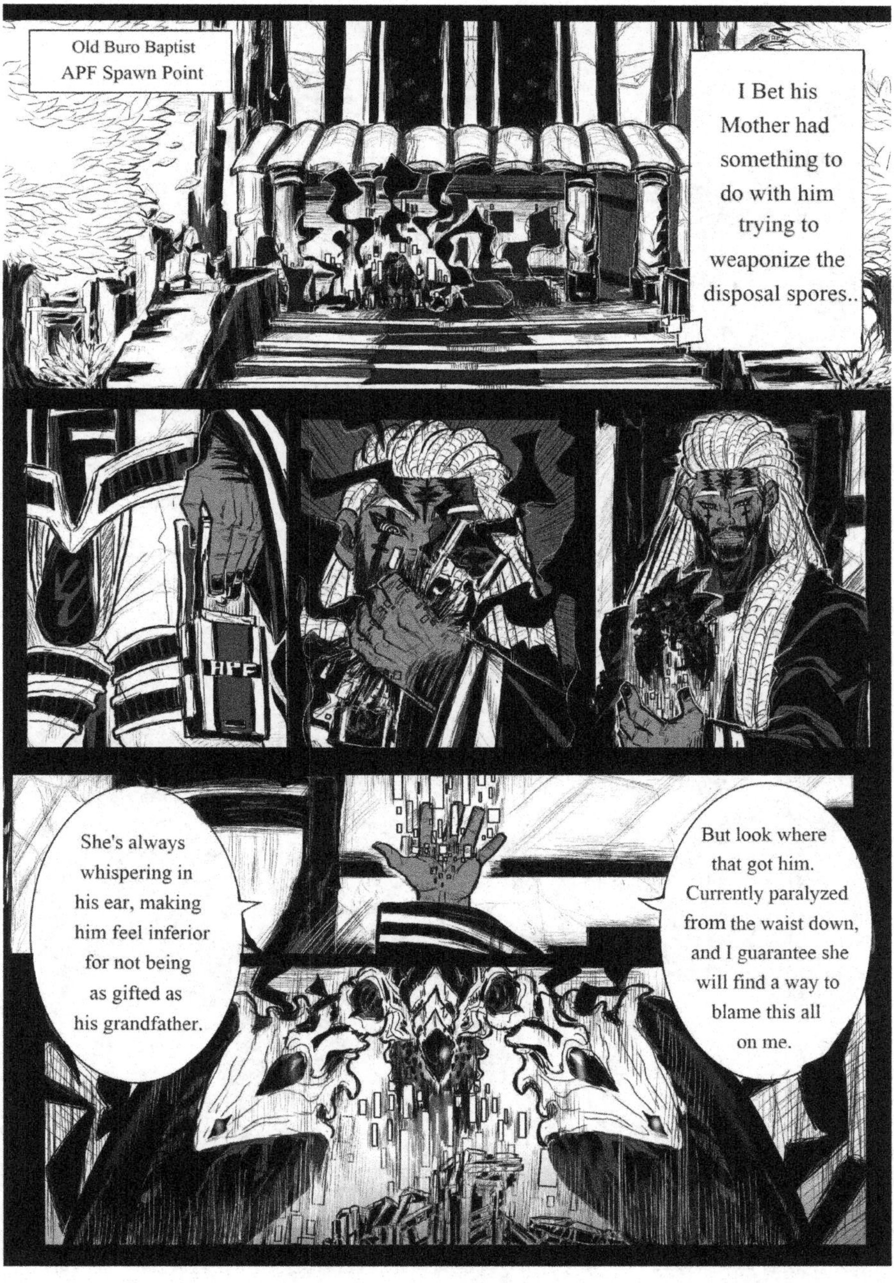
Old Buro Baptist
APF Spawn Point
I Bet his Mother had something to do with him trying to weaponize the disposal spores..
APF
She's always whispering in his ear, making him feel inferior for not being as gifted as his grandfather.
But look where that got him. Currently paralyzed from the waist down, and I guarantee she will find a way to blame this all on me.

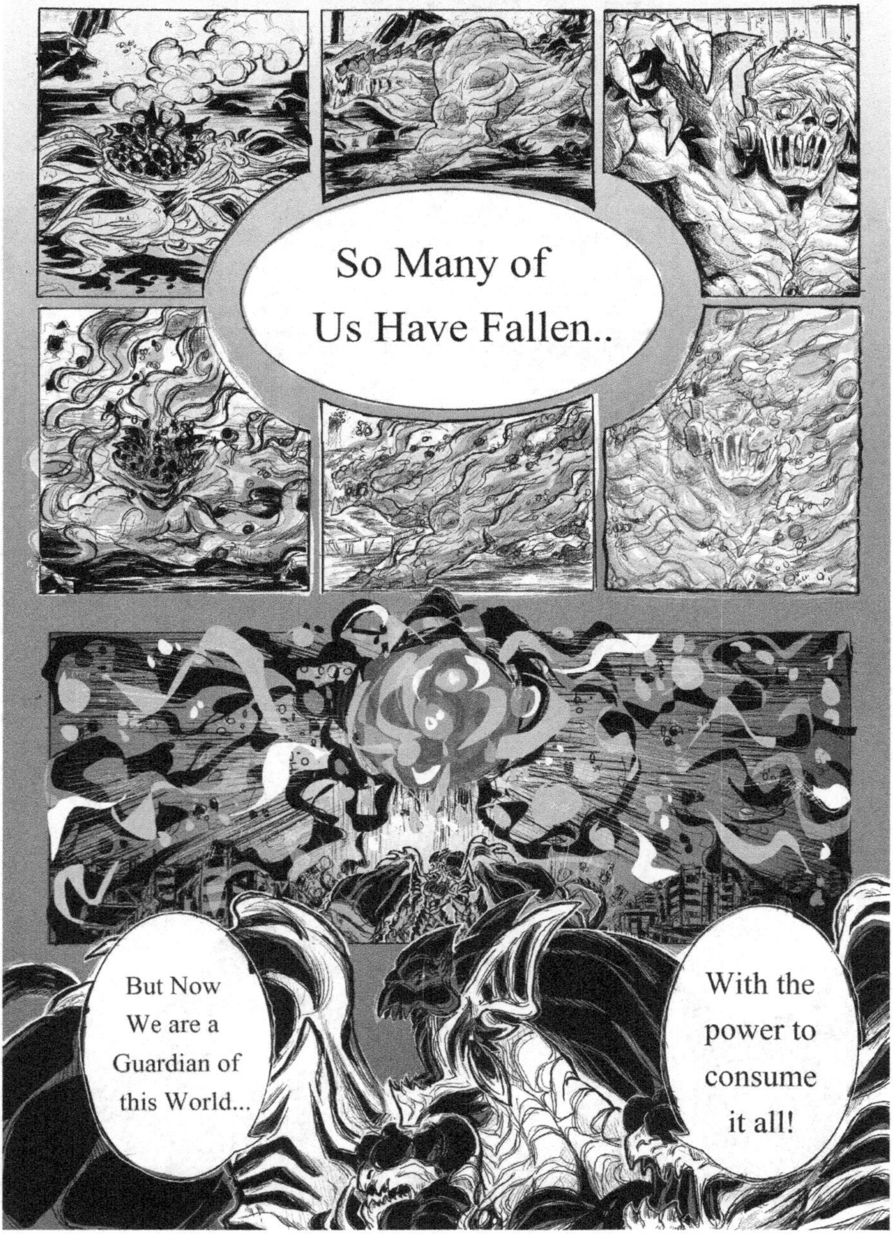
So Many of Us Have Fallen..
But Now We are a Guardian of this World...
With the power to consume it all!

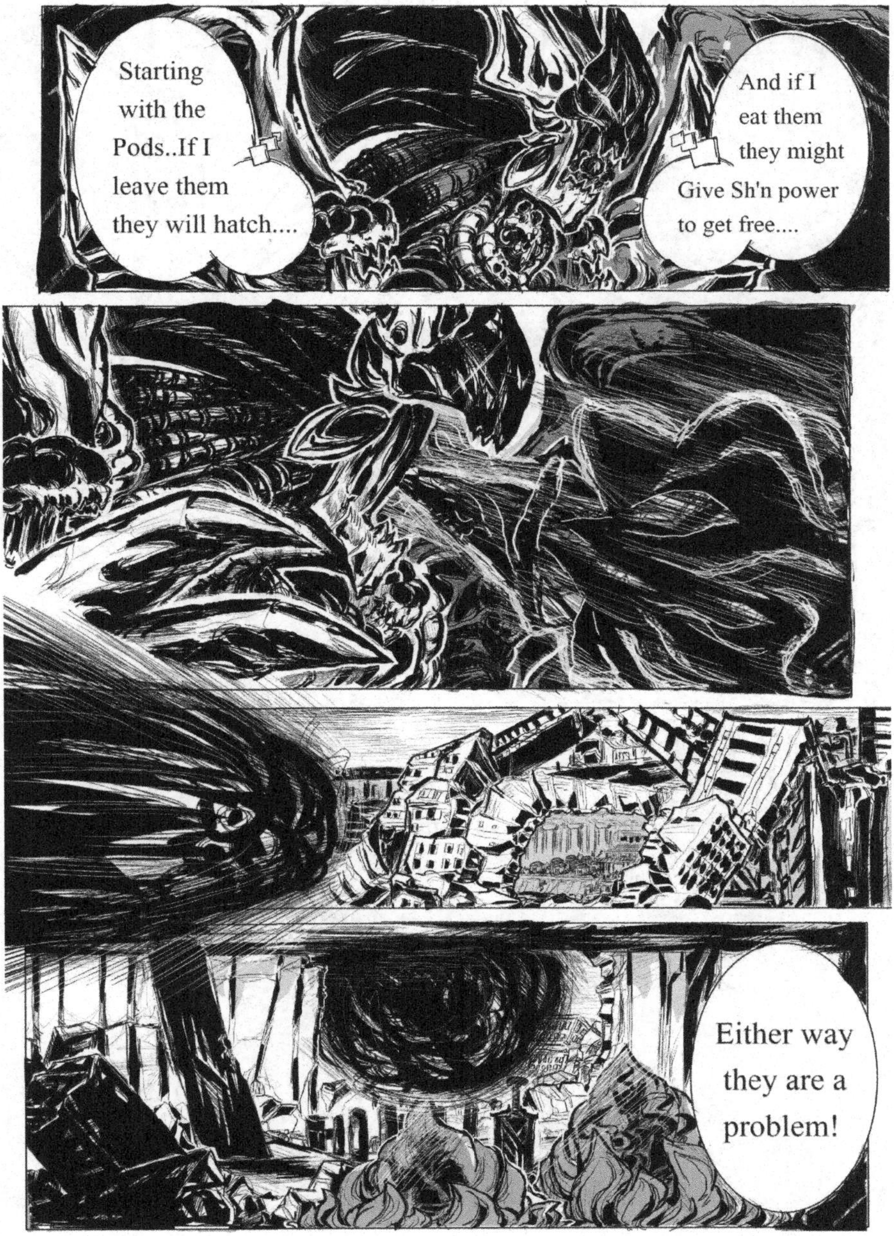
Starting with the Pods..If I leave them they will hatch....
And if I eat them they might Give Sh'n power to get free....
Either way they are a problem!

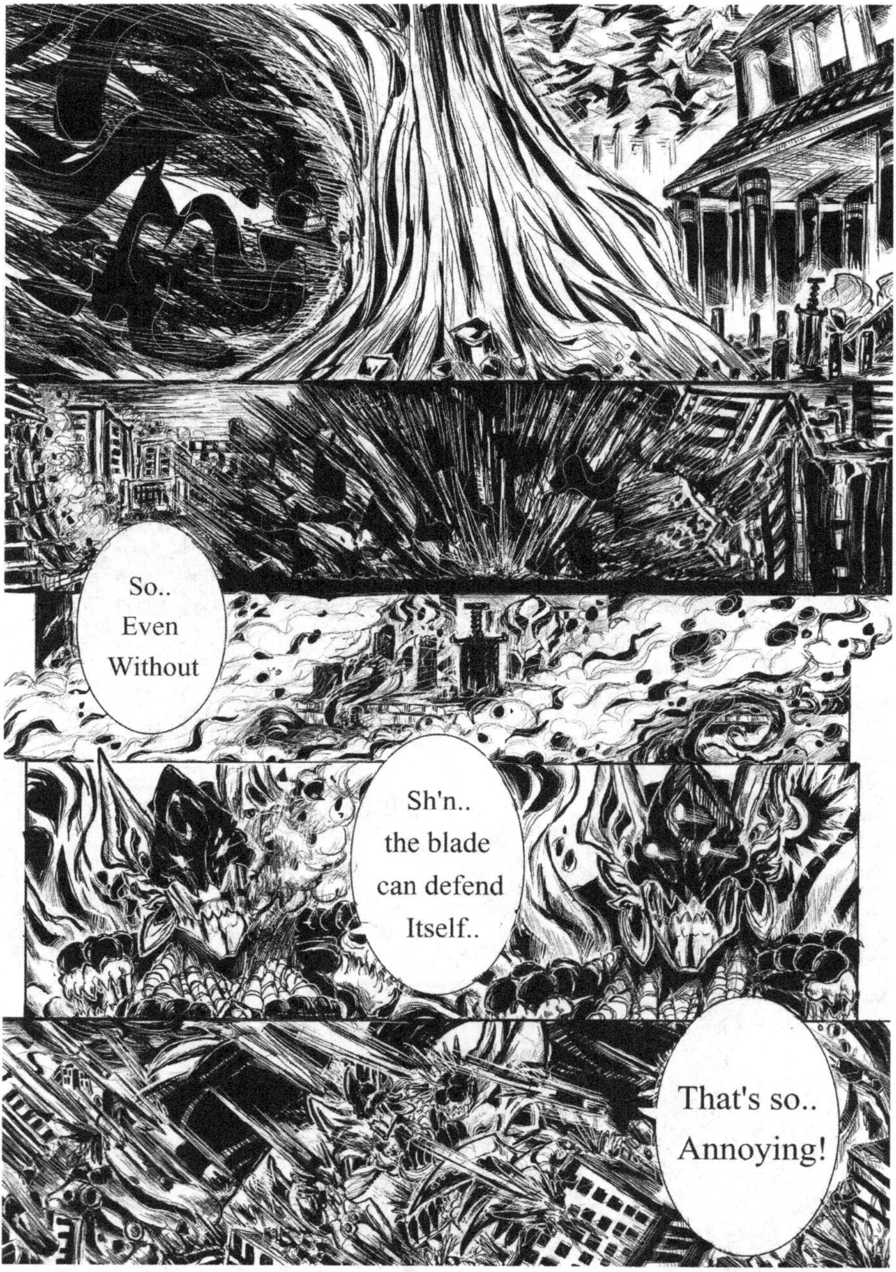
So.. Even Without
Sh'n.. the blade can defend Itself..
That's so.. Annoying!

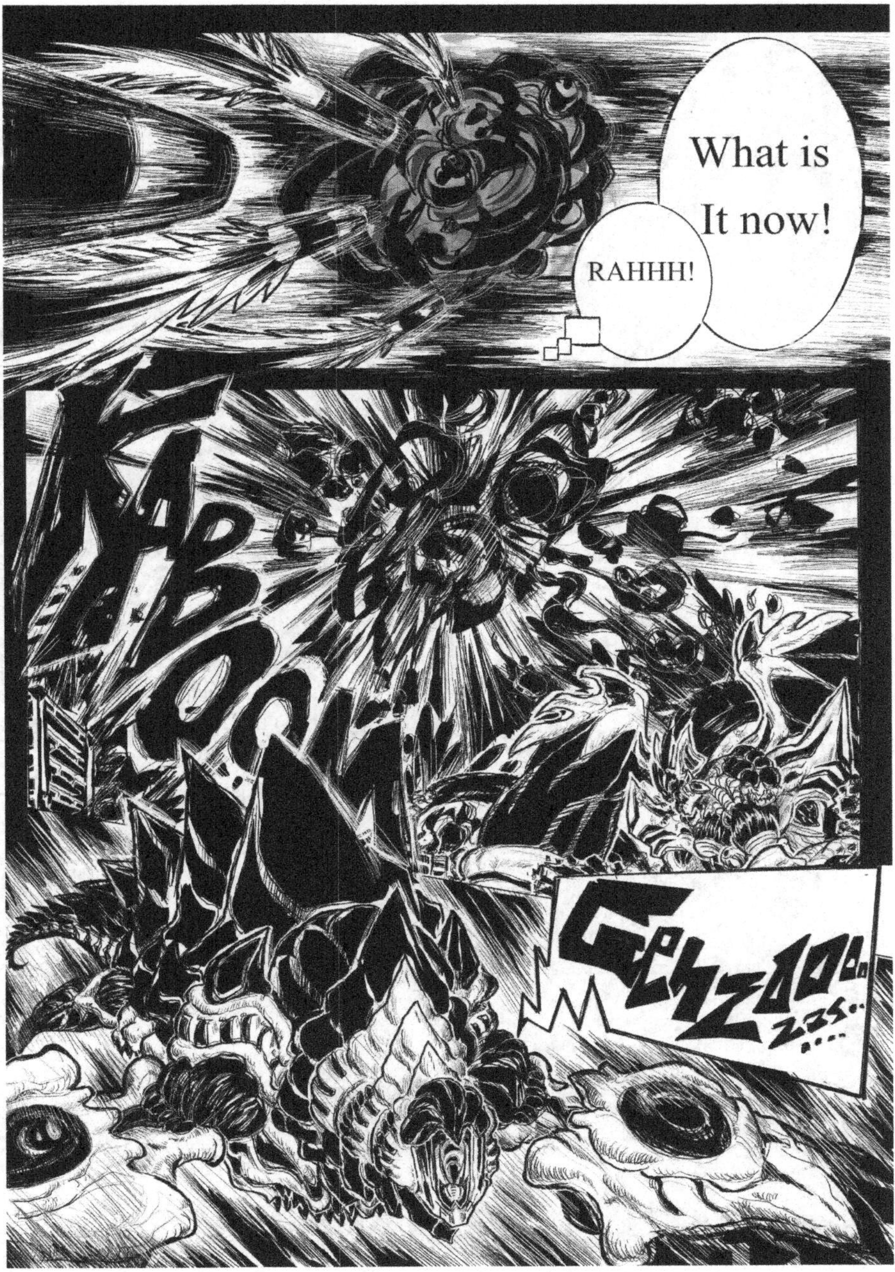
What is
It now!
RAHHH!
KABOOM

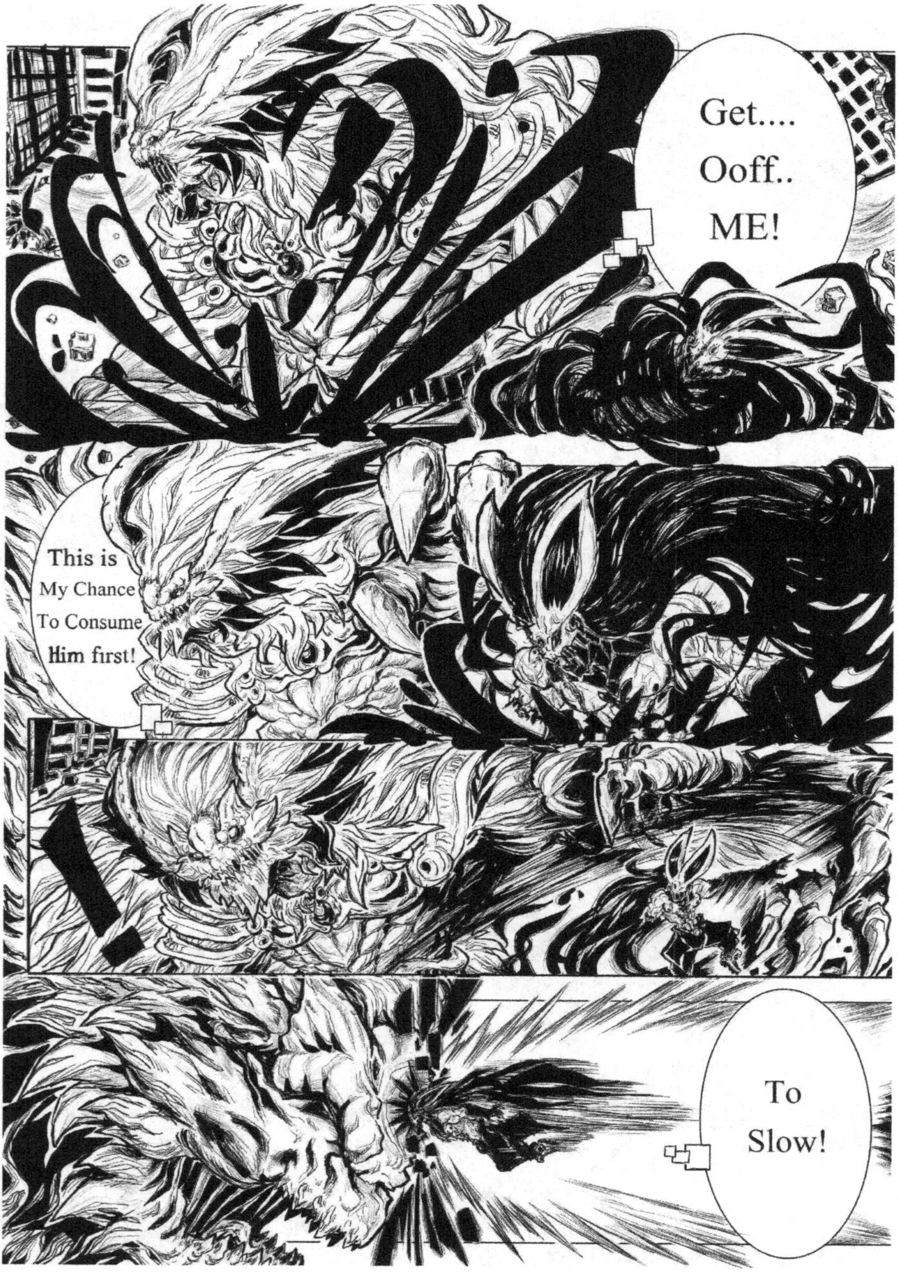
Get....
Ooff..
ME!
This is
My Chance
To Consume
Him first!
To
Slow!

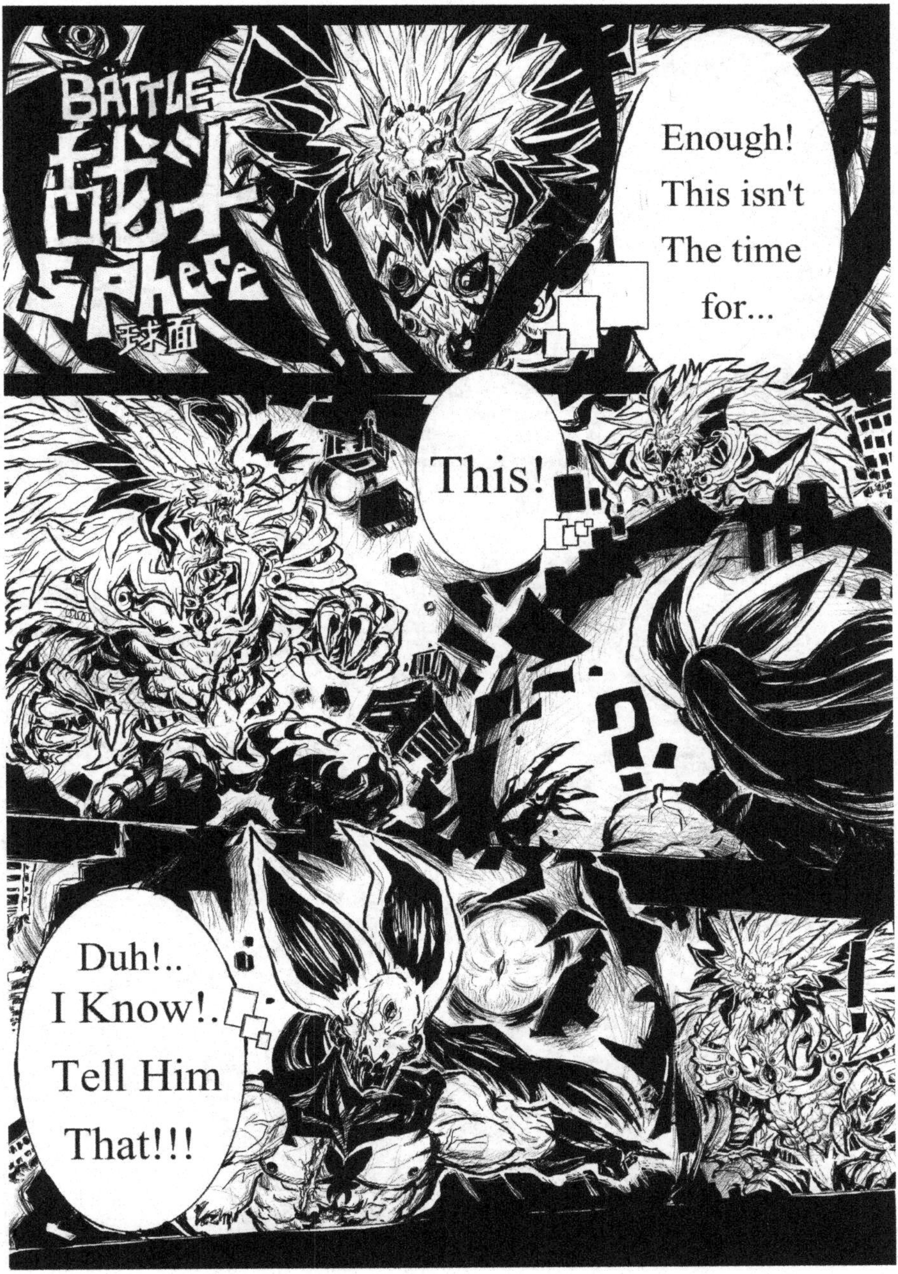
BATTLE
Sphere
Enough! This isn't The time for...
This!
?
Duh!.. I Know!.. Tell Him That!!!
!

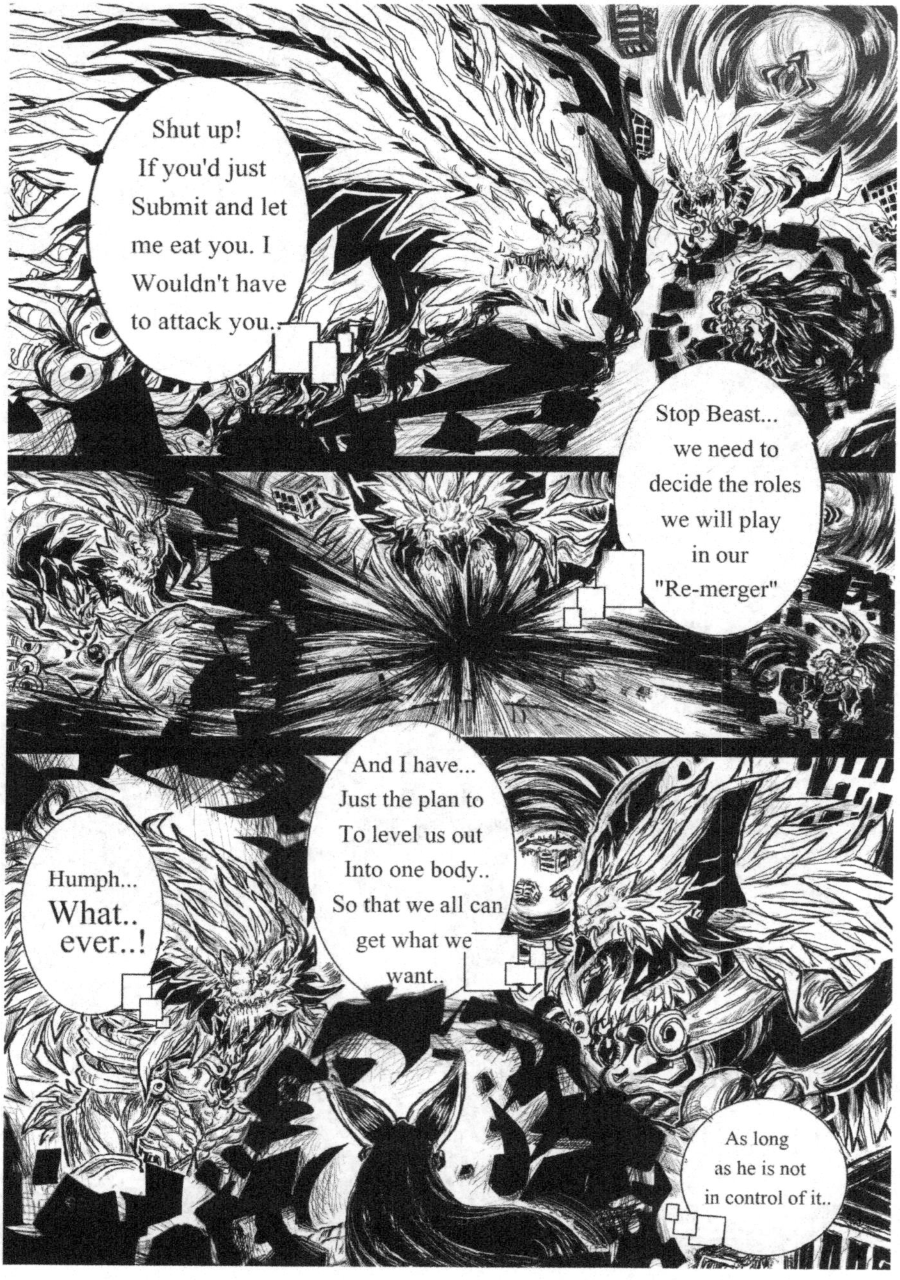
Shut up! If you'd just Submit and let me eat you. I Wouldn't have to attack you..
Stop Beast... we need to decide the roles we will play in our "Re-merger"
Humph... What.. ever..!
And I have... Just the plan to To level us out Into one body.. So that we all can get what we want..
As long as he is not in control of it..

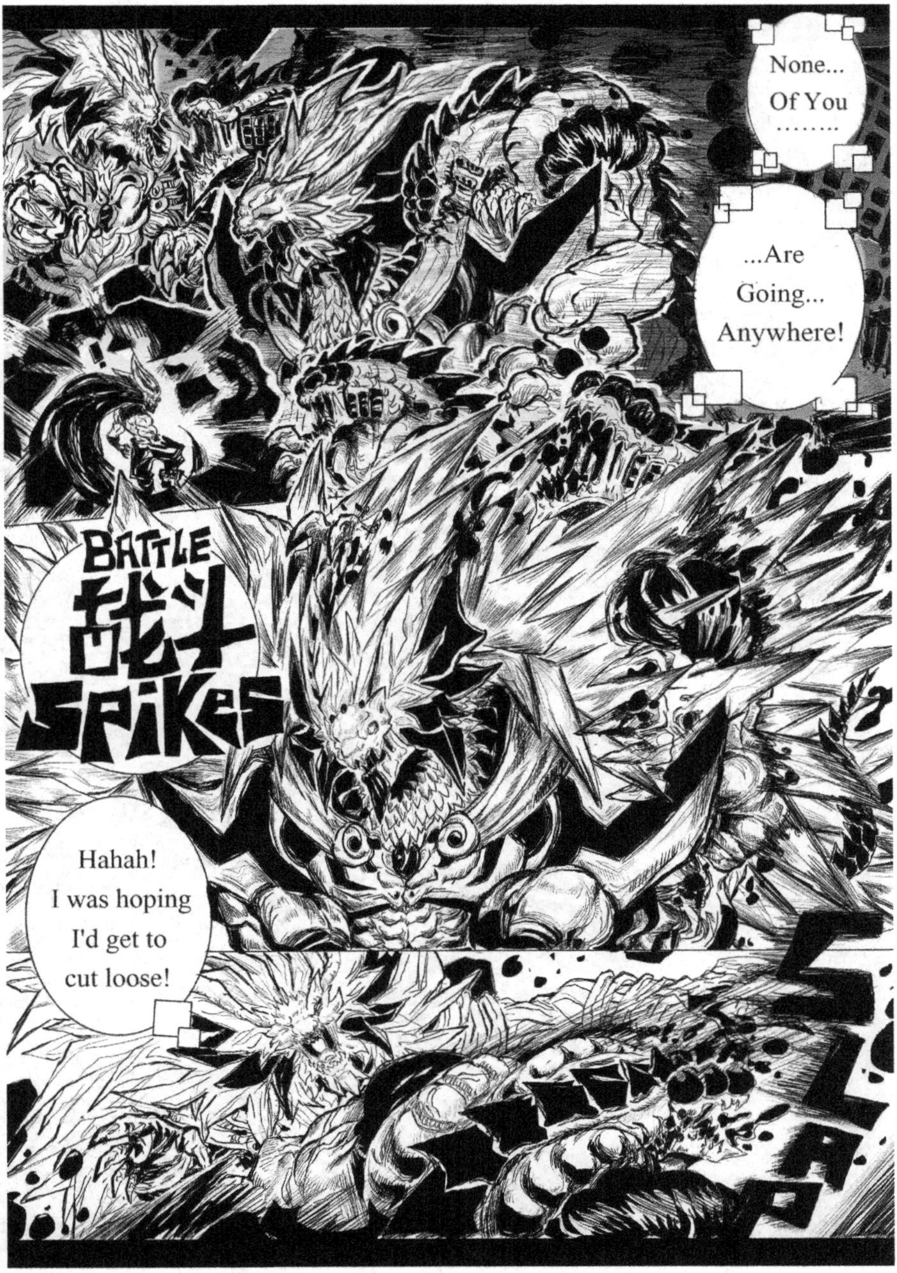
None... Of You ....
...Are Going... Anywhere!
!
BATTLE 战斗 SPIKES
Hahah! I was hoping I'd get to cut loose!
SLAP

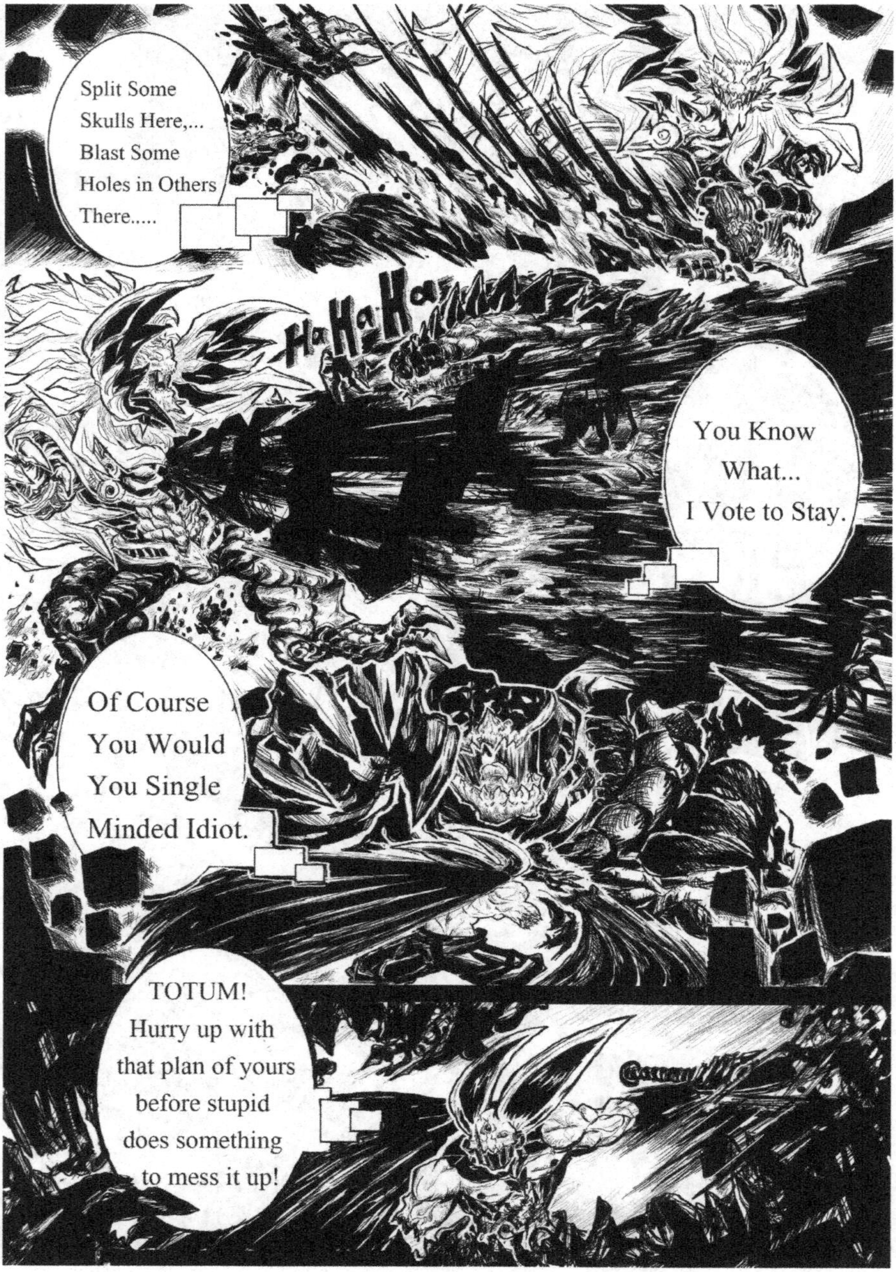
Split Some Skulls Here,... Blast Some Holes in Others There.....
HaHaHa
You Know What... I Vote to Stay.
Of Course You Would You Single Minded Idiot.
TOTUM! Hurry up with that plan of yours before stupid does something to mess it up!

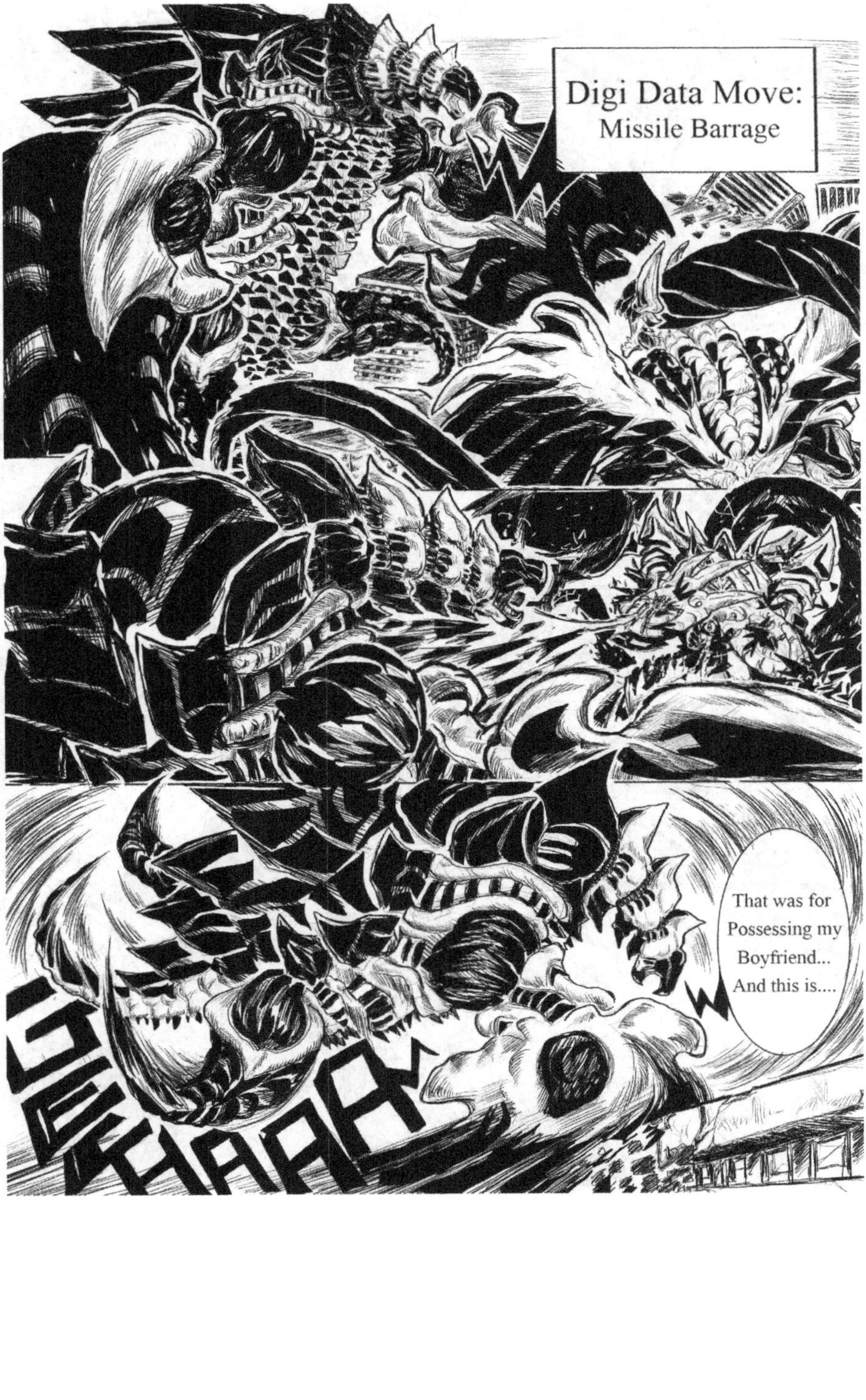
Digi Data Move:
Missile Barrage
That was for Possessing my Boyfriend... And this is....

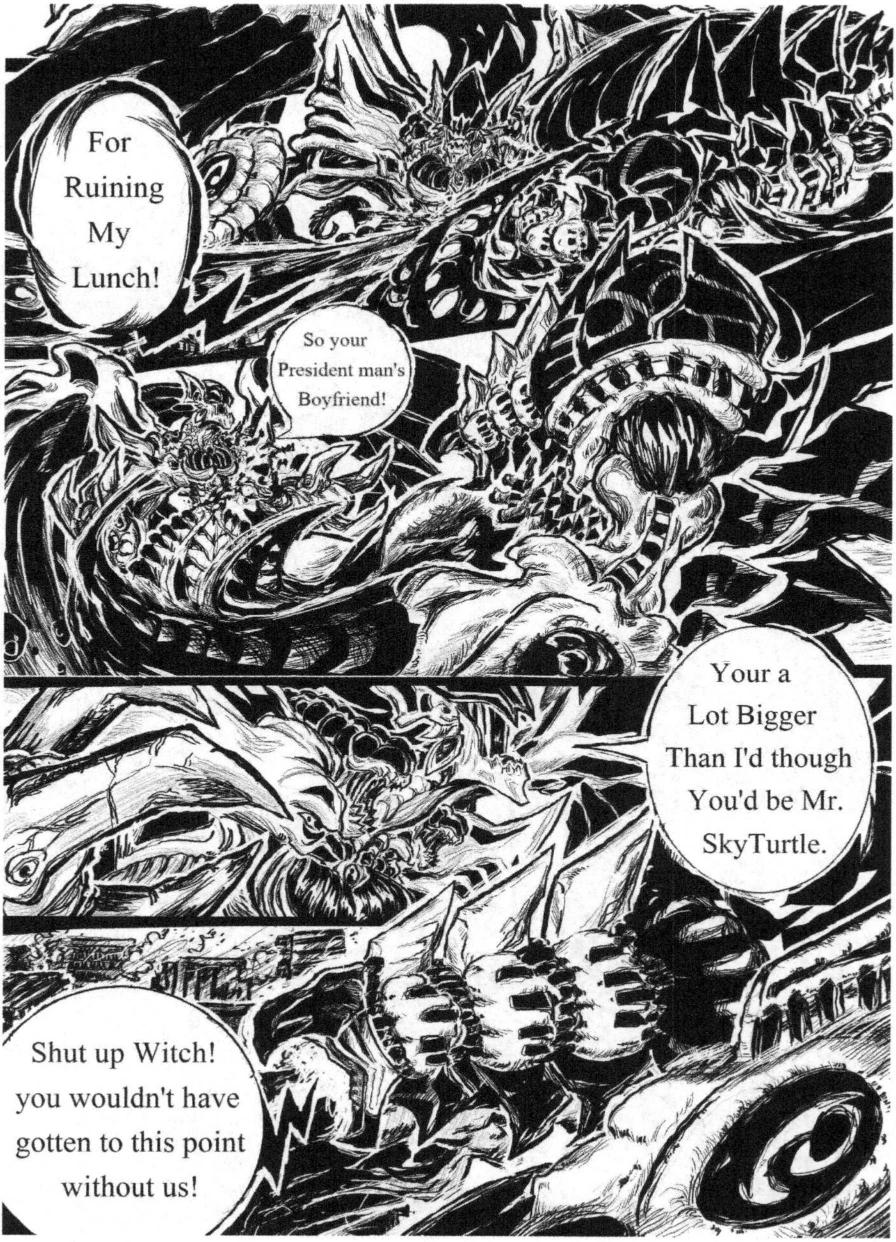
For Ruining My Lunch!
So your President man's Boyfriend!
Your a Lot Bigger Than I'd though You'd be Mr. SkyTurtle.
Shut up Witch! you wouldn't have gotten to this point without us!

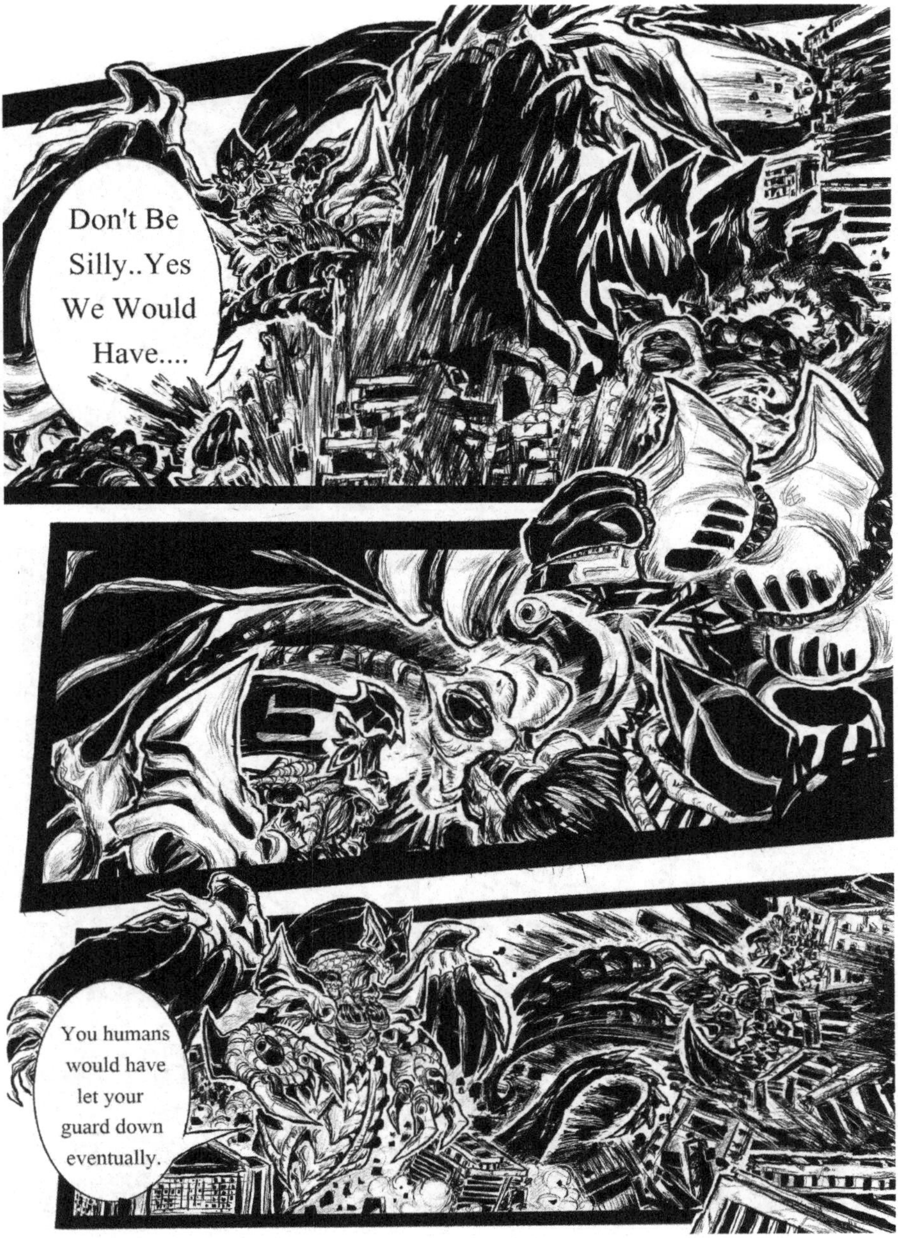
Don't Be Silly..Yes We Would Have....
You humans would have let your guard down eventually.

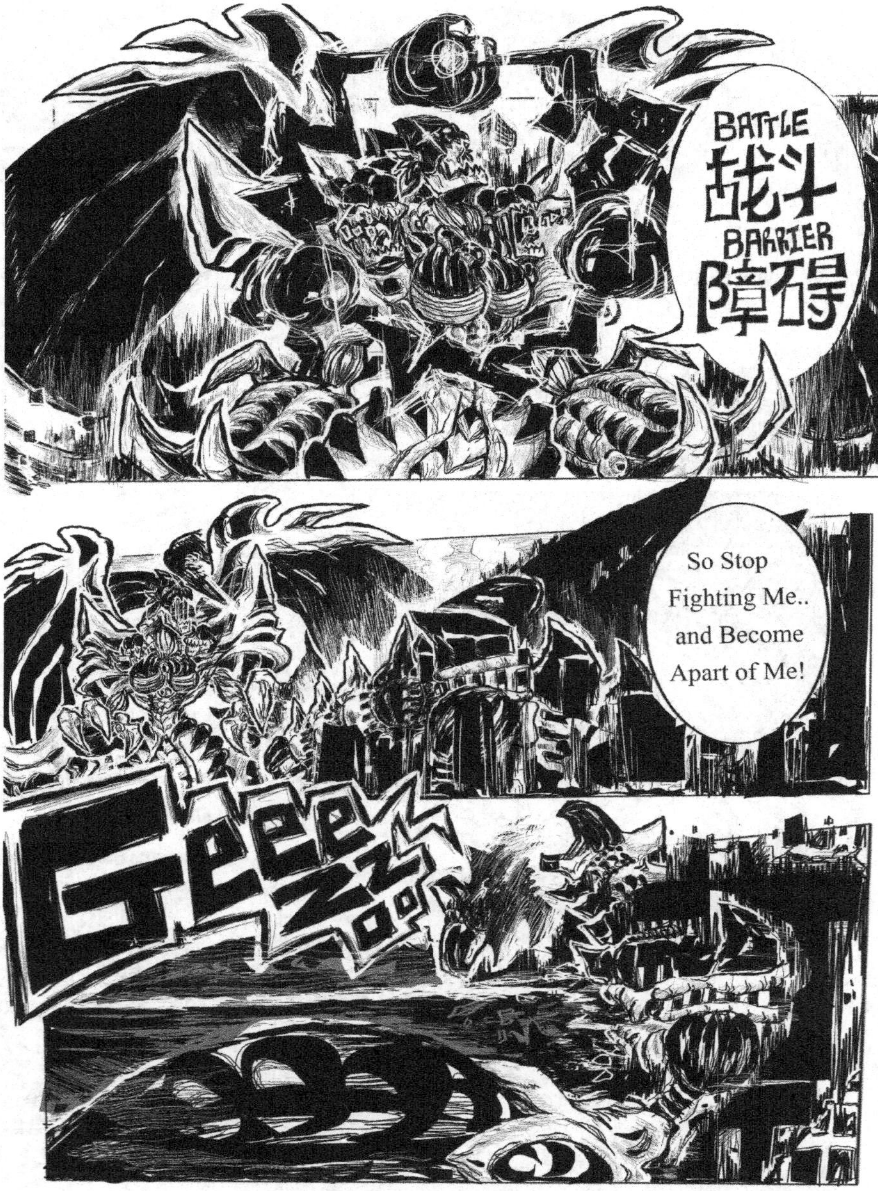
BATTLE 战斗 BARRIER 障碍
So Stop Fighting Me.. and Become Apart of Me!
Geeezzoo

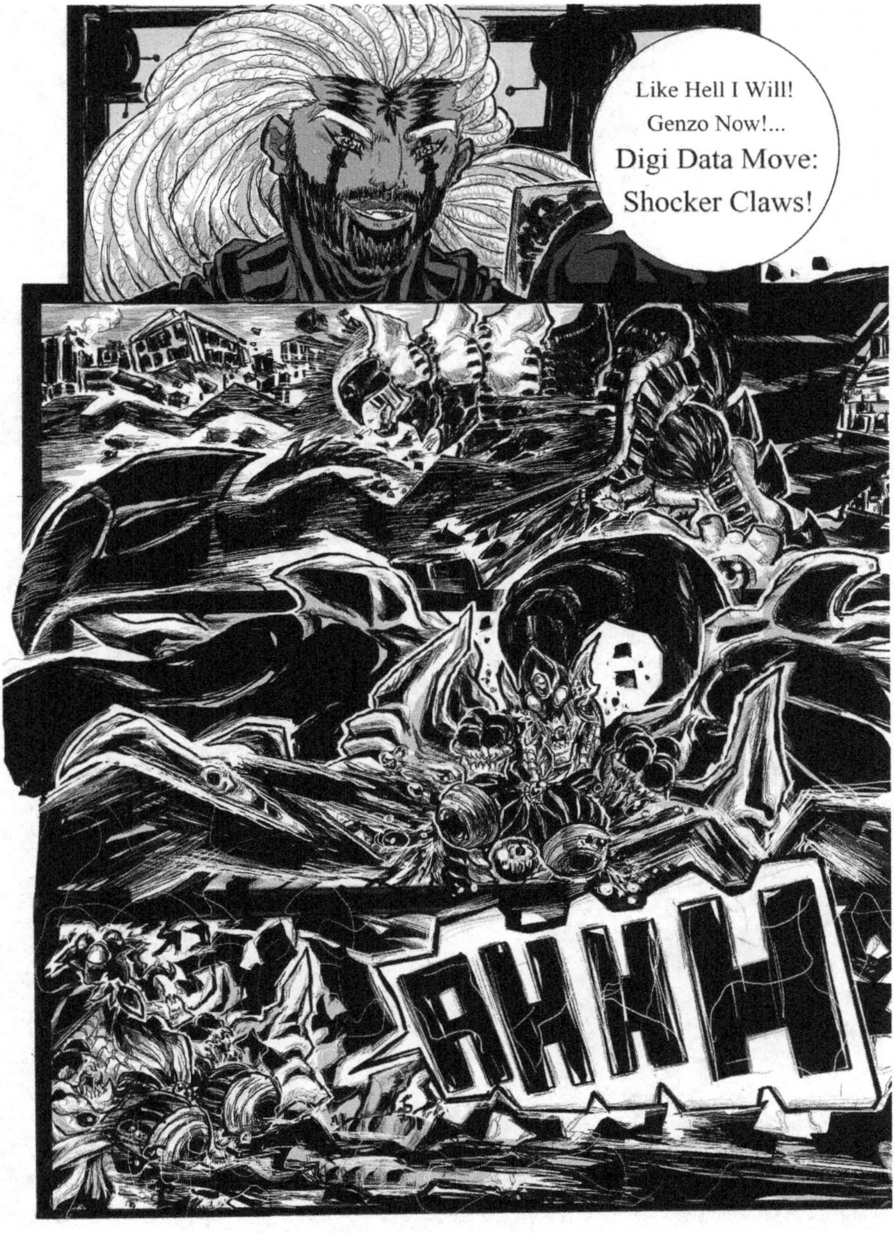
Like Hell I Will!
Genzo Now!...
Digi Data Move:
Shocker Claws!

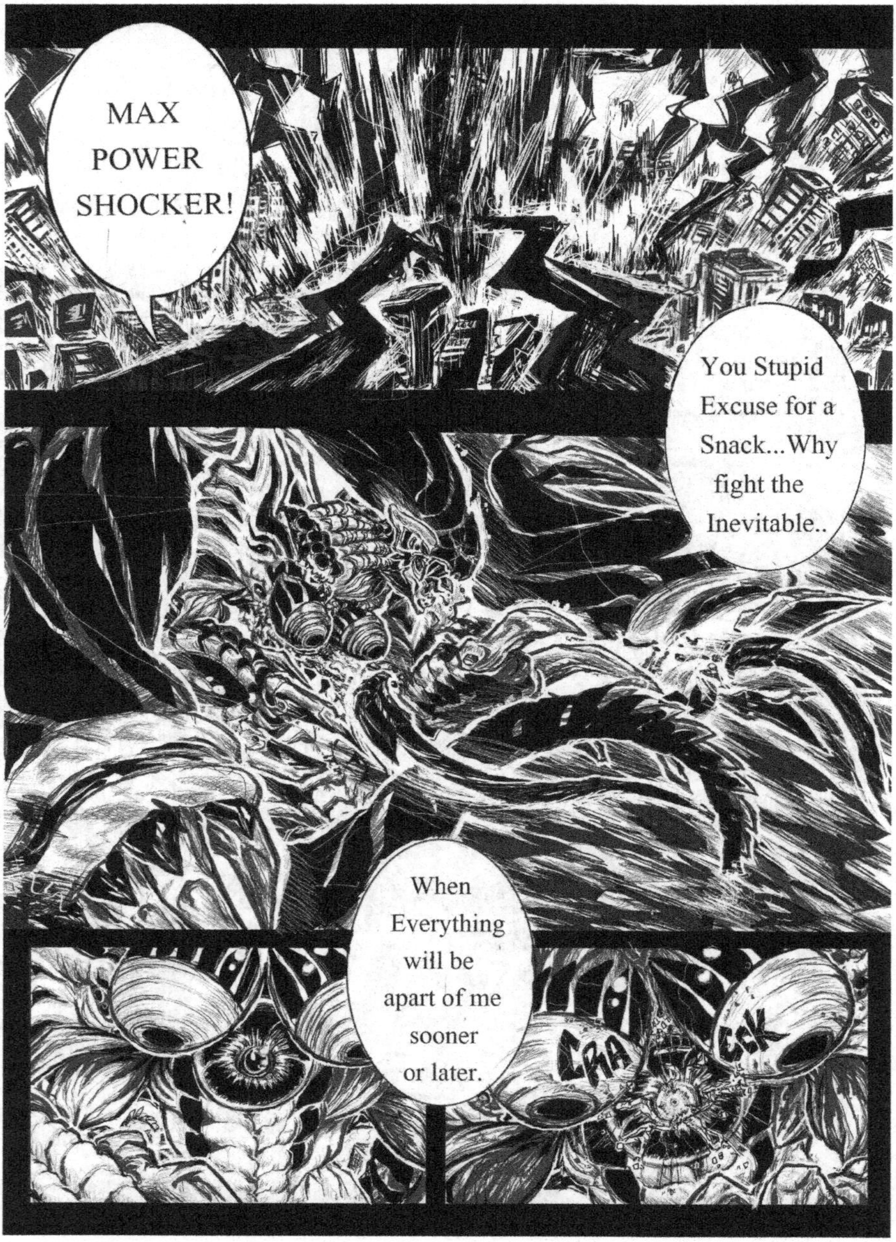
MAX POWER SHOCKER!
You Stupid Excuse for a Snack...Why fight the Inevitable..
When Everything will be apart of me sooner or later.
CRA CCK

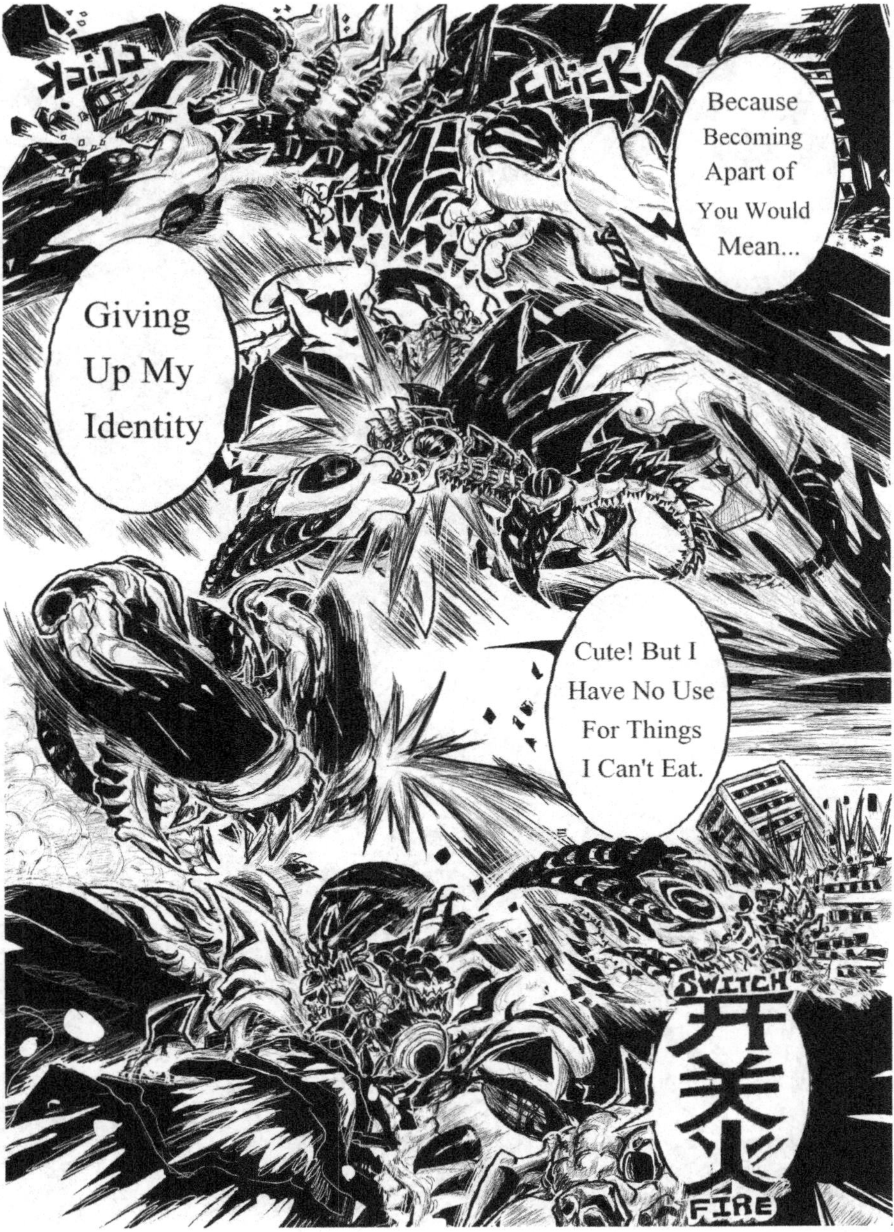
CLICK
CLICK
Because Becoming Apart of You Would Mean...
Giving Up My Identity
Cute! But I Have No Use For Things I Can't Eat.
SWITCH
FIRE

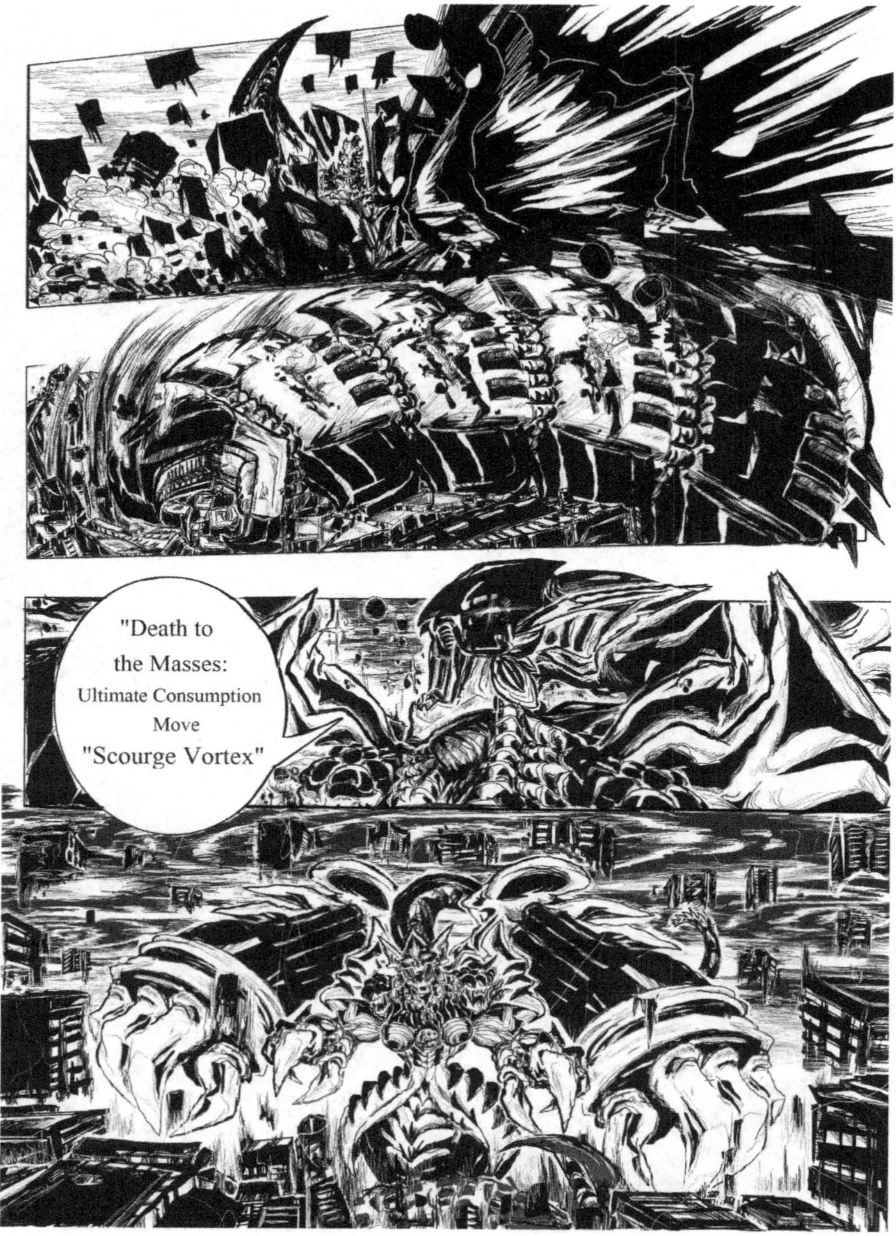
"Death to the Masses: Ultimate Consumption Move "Scourge Vortex"

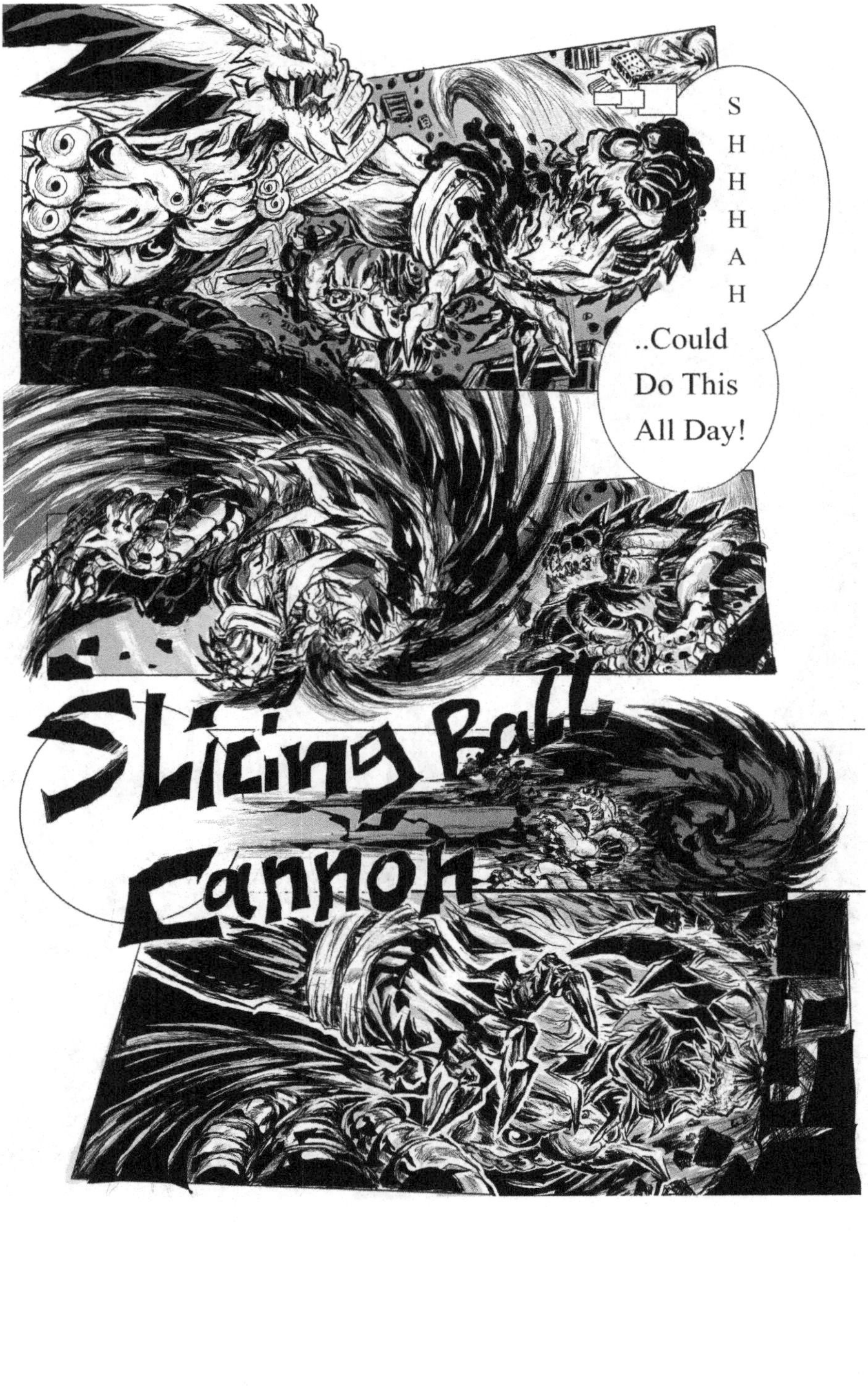
SHHHAH
..Could Do This All Day!
Slicing Ball Cannon

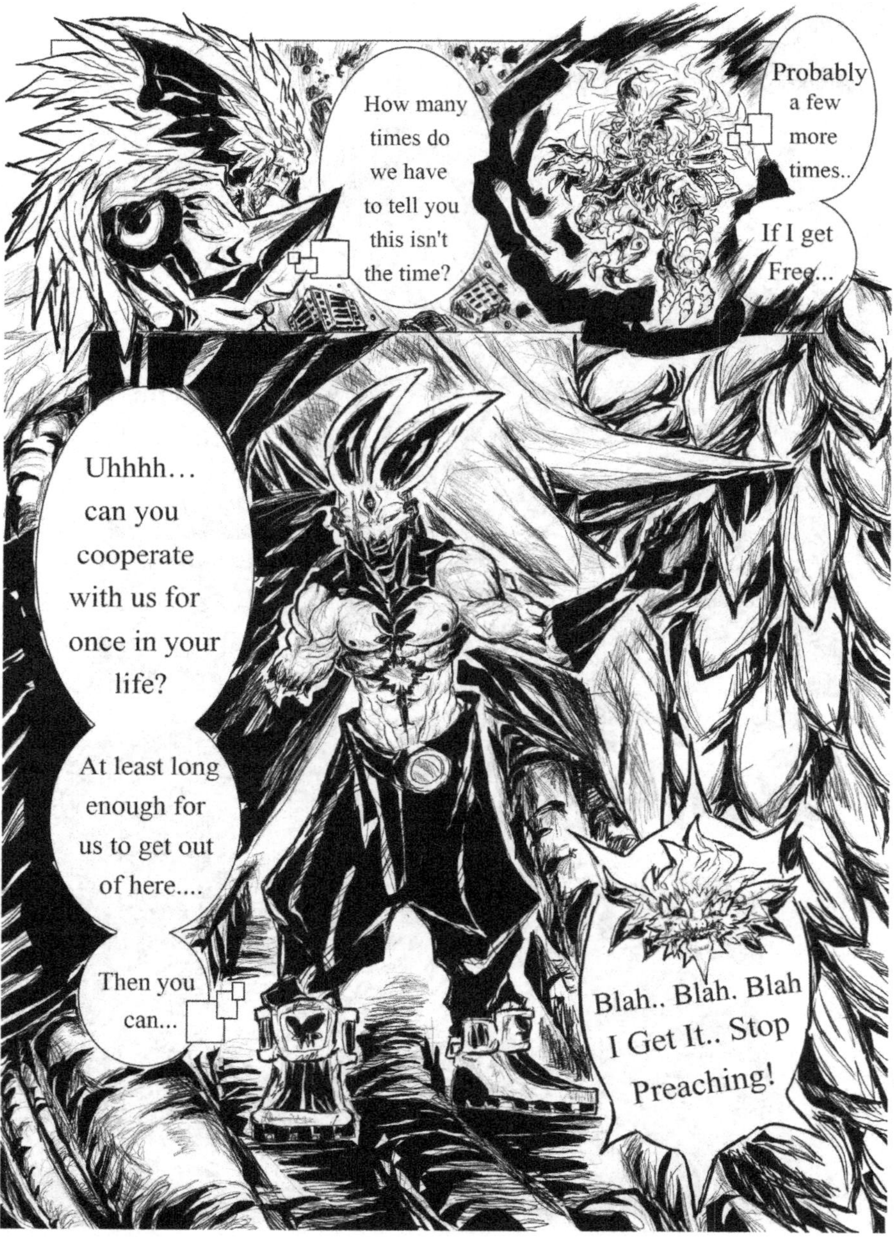
How many times do we have to tell you this isn't the time?
Probably a few more times..
If I get Free...
Uhhhh… can you cooperate with us for once in your life?
At least long enough for us to get out of here....
Then you can...
Blah.. Blah. Blah I Get It.. Stop Preaching!

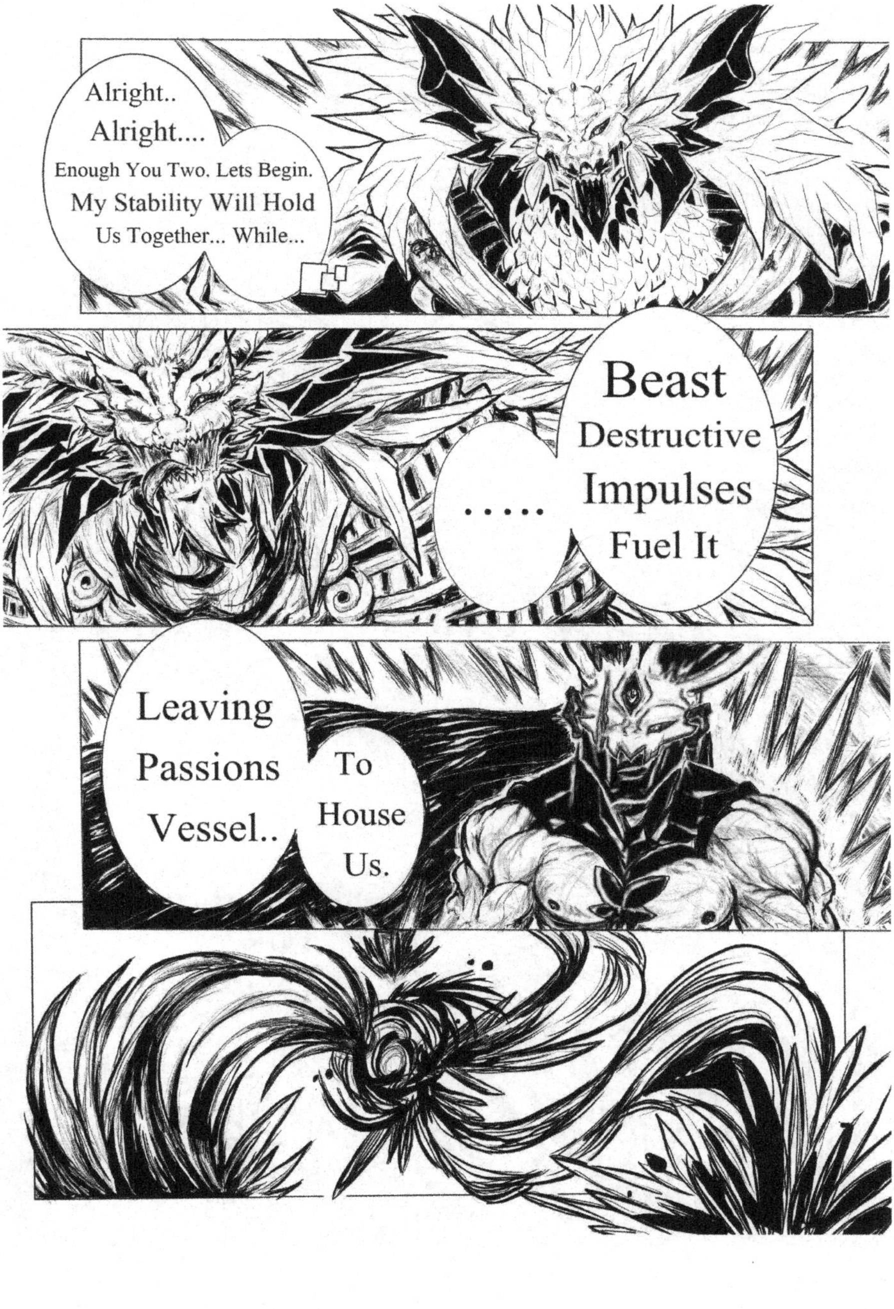
Alright..
Alright....
Enough You Two. Lets Begin.
My Stability Will Hold
Us Together... While...
.....
Beast
Destructive
Impulses
Fuel It
Leaving
Passions
Vessel..
To
House
Us.

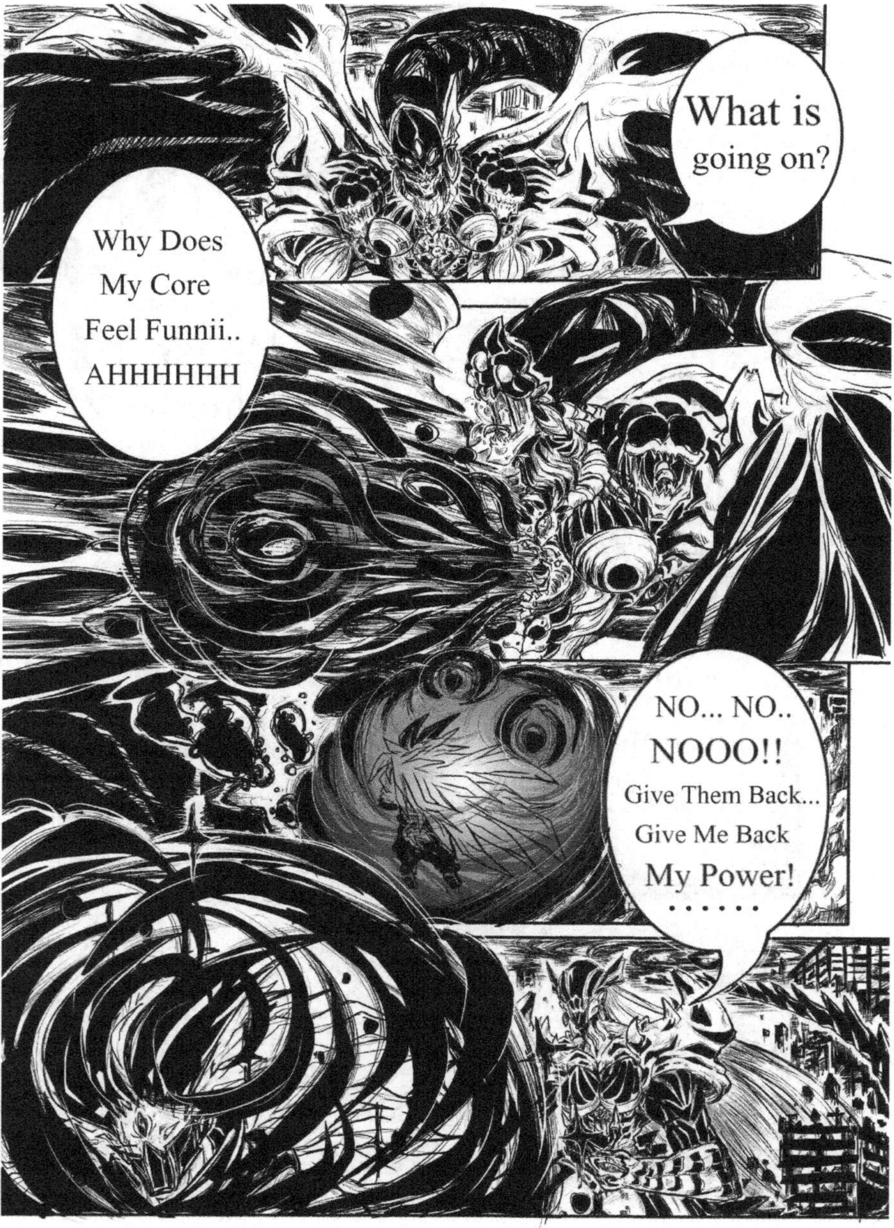
What is going on?
Why Does My Core Feel Funnii.. AHHHHHH
NO... NO.. NOOO!! Give Them Back... Give Me Back My Power! ......

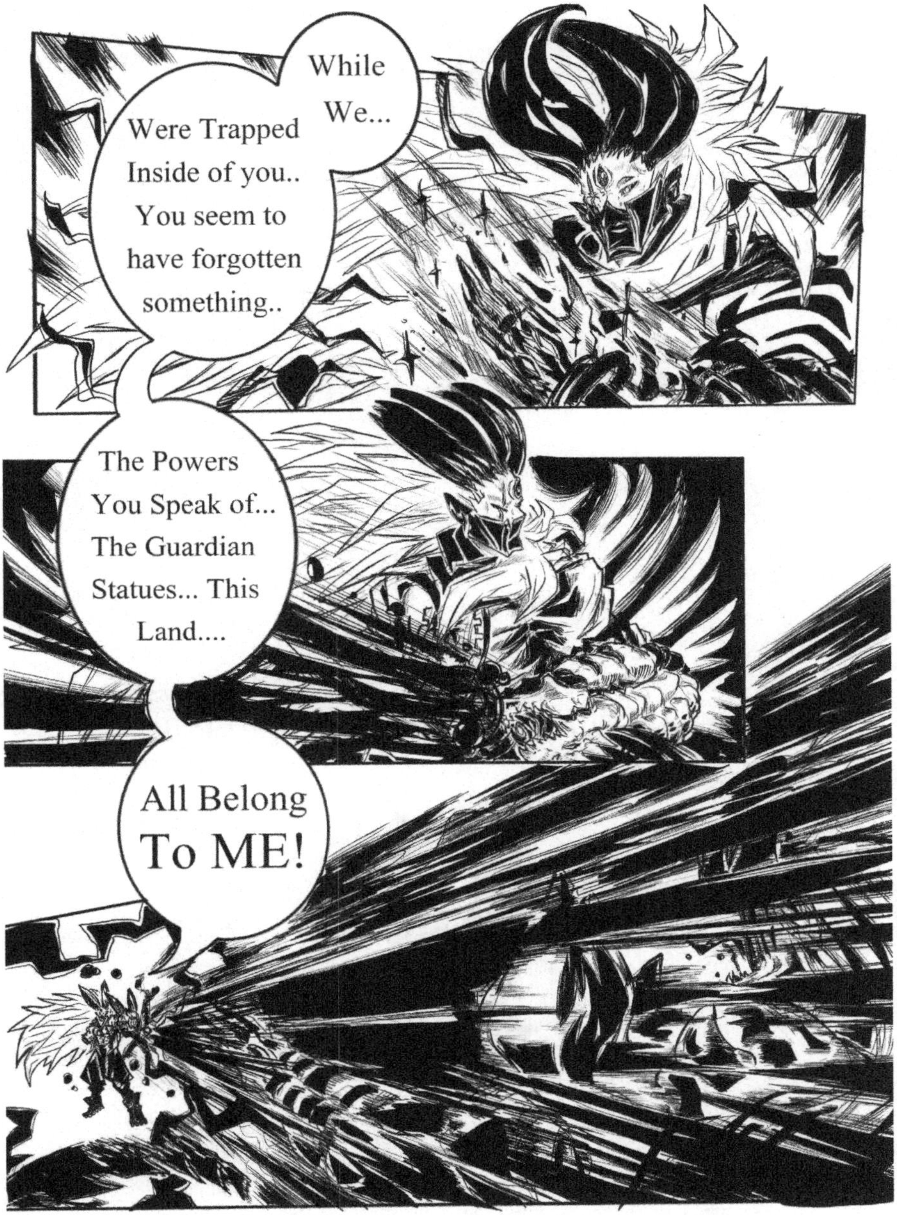
While We...
Were Trapped Inside of you.. You seem to have forgotten something..
The Powers You Speak of... The Guardian Statues... This Land....
All Belong To ME!

https://www.linkedin.com/in/robert-christopher-dilworth-193a95106/

https://www.webtoons.com/en/challenge/shn-volume-one/list?title_no=691364

The Story of Sh'n.
"The Rabbit God."
Guardian Aspect of The
Northern Hemisphere.

Made in the USA
Coppell, TX
09 April 2022

76283412R00056